Yankees vs. Cardinals

Souvenir ~ Program

MILLER J. HUGGINS
New York Yankees

BILL McKECHNIE
St. Louis Cardinals

Worlds Championship Series, 1928

Yankee Stadium – New York
Price 25 cents

HARRY M. STEVENS, Inc., Publisher

WORLD'S SERIES

1932

CHICAGO CUBS
vs.
NEW YORK YANKEES

CHICAGO
NATIONAL
LEAGUE
BALL CLUB

WRIGLEY FIELD

Souvenir
SCORE CARD
25¢

UNITED·STATES·OF·AMERICA
E
PLURIBUS
UNUM

WORLD
SERIES

Giants vs Yankees
1936

Official Program 25¢

Joe DiMaggio

WORLD
SERIES

1937
YANKEES
vs
GIANTS
OFFICIAL
PROGRAM
25¢

PRICE 25¢

WORLDS 193?
SERIES

Yankees 49

HOME OF CHAMPIONS

YANKEE STADIUM

'22 '23 '26 '27
'32 '28
'36 '37
'39 '38
'42 '43 '47 '49

1950

1951 WORLD SERIES

NEW YORK

Giants

VS

NEW YORK

Yankees

1876
NATIONAL
1951
OFFICIAL PROGRAM FIFTY CENTS

AMERICAN
1901 · 1951
GOLDEN
ANNIVERSARY

Yankees

WORLD 1952 SERIES

Dodgers

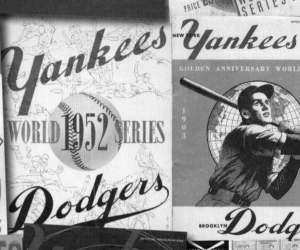

New York Yankees

GOLDEN ANNIVERSARY WORLD S

1903

Brooklyn Dodge

WORLD SERIES

Dodgers

LD SERIES 1961

"Home Of Champions"

MANAGER
RALPH HOUK

NKEES CINCINNATI REDS

WORLD SERIES 1962
Yankee Stadium

62

NEW YORK
YANKEES
vs
SAN FRANCISCO
GIANTS

WORLD SERIES

1963

DODGERS YANKEES

OFFICIAL
SOUVENIR PROGRAM

Yankees

WORLD SERIES

1964 WORLD SERIES

Cardinals

YANKEE STADIUM

WORLD SERIES 1976

World Series

Braves

World Series
2000

The
FALL
CLASSIC

MAJOR LEAGUE BASEBALL
OFFICIAL
PROGRAM

World Series
2001

Major League Baseball
OFFICIAL PROGRAM

MAJOR LEAGUE BASEBALL OFFICIAL PROGR

3

WORLD
SERIES
100th ANNIVERSARY
2003

1963
RAIN CHECK

MAJOR LEAGUE BASEBALL
OFFICIAL PROGRAM

WORLD
SERIES
20 09
Fall Classic

PHILADELPHIA PHILLIES
vs.
NEW YORK YANKEES

Phillies

YANKEE CLASSICS

WORLD SERIES MAGIC FROM THE BRONX BOMBERS
— 1921 TO TODAY —

INCLUDES A DVD OF GREAT MOMENTS FROM THE CLASSIC ERA OF THE WORLD SERIES
NARRATED BY
REGGIE JACKSON

LES KRANTZ
AUTHOR OF *YANKEE STADIUM: A TRIBUTE*

FOREWORD BY WHITEY FORD

MVP
BOOKS

To Uncle Harry, in appreciation of those Yankee Stadium tickets and my very first visit to the sanctuary.

Contributing writers: Paul Adomites, David Fischer, David Kaplan, Matt Silverman, Marty Strasen

First published in 2010 by MVP Books, an imprint of MBI Publishing Company and the Quayside Publishing Group, 400 First Avenue North, Suite 300, Minneapolis, MN 55401 USA.

MVP Books titles are also available at discounts in bulk quantity for industrial or sales-promotional use. For details write to Special Sales Manager at Quayside Publishing Group, 400 First Avenue North, Suite 300, Minneapolis, MN 55401 USA.

To find out more about our books, visit us online at www.mvpbooks.com.

ISBN-13: 978-0-7603-4019-6

Library of Congress Cataloging-in-Publication Data is available.

Produced by Facts That Matter, Inc.
Designed by Julie Nor/Flair Studio

Printed in China by PWGS

Photo Credits

AP Images: 37, 41, 59, 60 right, 61 left, 66, 70 left, 73, 75, 80, 87, 94, 99 left, 114, 115 top, 120, 124 left, 127, 133, 134; Tom Fitzsimmons 67 right; Edward S. Kitch 55; John Rooney 111.

Getty Images: AFP/Henny Ray Abrams 152; AFP/Matt Campbell 148 top; AFP/Timothy A. Clary 153 bottom, 162; AFP/Jeff Haynes 149, 155; AFP/Stan Honda 161; Archive photos 78 left; Archive Photos/APA 57 bottom; Archive Photos/New York Times Co. 53 top, 109; Al Bello, 157 bottom, 166, 167 bottom right, 171 bottom; Bruce Bennett 15, 45, 105; Matt Campbell 163; Mark Cunningham 145; Diamond Images 17 left, 42 left, 46, 50 right, 51, 61 right, 78 right, 91, 110 left; Diamond Images/Kidwiler Collection 38, 92 left; Diamond Images/Olen Collection 77, 173; Stephen Dunn 142; Focus on Sport 138; Vincent Laforet 147; Nick Laham 169; V. J. Lovero 141; New York Daily News 10 right, 13 left, 27 top, 49, 63, 69, 70 right, 113, 130, 131, 144 left, 151, 156, 159, 160 left, 165, 170; Robert Riger 117; Rogers Photo Archive 30 left, 71, 102 top; Sports Illustrated/James Drake 135 left; Sports Illustrated/Walter Iooss Jr. 119, 128 left; Sports Illustrated/Mark Kauffman 88; Sports Illustrated/Heinz Kluetmeier 129, 135 right; Sports Illustrated/Richard Mackson 139 bottom; Sports Illustrated/Richard Meek 97; Sports Illustrated/Manny Millan 137; Sports Illustrated/Marvin E. Newman 106; Sports Illustrated/Herb Scharfman 107 top, 123; Sports Illustrated/Tony Triolo 125; Sports Illustrated/John G. Zimmerman 92 right; Chuck Solomon 143; Al Tielemans 167 bottom left; Time & Life Pictures/Henry Groskinsky 121 bottom; Time & Life Pictures/Francis Miller 79, 101, 103; Transcendental Graphics vii, 13 right, 17 right, 19 top, 21, 22 top, 23, 25, 26, 31, 33, 34, 50 left, 60 left, 62, 84 top, 85, 95, 98; Chris Trotman vi.

National Baseball Hall of Fame and Museum: 9, 10 left, 29.

Front cover (left to right): Babe Ruth, Transcendental Graphics/Getty Images; Whitey Ford, Focus on Sport/Getty Images; Commissioner's Trophy, Jim McIsaac/Getty Images; Reggie Jackson, Focus on Sport/Getty Images; Derek Jeter: AFP/Timothy A. Clary/Getty Images. **Back cover:** Murray Becker/AP Images.

ACKNOWLEDGMENTS

The author would like to express his gratitude to the outstanding writers who contributed to this book: Paul Adomites, who has authored many baseball history books including *Babe Ruth: His Life and Times*; Dave Kaplan, author of *For the Love of the Yankees* and coauthor of multiple books with Yogi Berra; David Fischer, who authored *A Yankee Stadium Scrapbook* and other books on the Bronx Bombers; veteran sportswriter Marty Strasen, who counts *Reel Baseball* among his 10 author credits; and Matt Silverman, former managing editor of *Total Baseball* and author of numerous baseball books.

I am particularly grateful to my publisher at MVP Books, Josh Leventhal, for his many wonderful suggestions regarding editorial content and design. He helped my staff and me take this book to a higher level, and I consider his "stamp" on this book to be a feather in my professional cap.

I'd like to express my gratitude to Yankees great Whitey Ford, the winningest pitcher in World Series history, who wrote the foreword for this book. Thanks, too, to the book's designer, Julie Nor, whose creative vision helped make Yankees history come alive.

A special thank-you goes to video editor Jack Piantino, who led the production of the DVD documentary that accompanies this book. Kudos to sports editor and historian Jake Veyhl, who fact-checked the text with a vengeance, and to Chris Smith and Marci McGrath, who provided the index. My appreciation goes out to Heritage Auctions (www.ha.com), which provided most of the nostalgic memorabilia images that adorn these pages.

I'd like to express my thanks to Reggie Jackson, narrator of the DVD documentary. Known for his fabled World Series heroics with the Yankees, Jackson impressed me with the professionalism and enthusiasm he brought to the reading of the script. Mr. October has not lost his zest for the game of baseball, and his love for the Yankees still runs deep. Reggie, it was a thrill! I'm also grateful to agent Matt Merola, who brought two of the greatest Yankees into this project: Reggie and Whitey.

CONTENTS

Whitey Ford, in 2009

FOREWORD BY WHITEY FORD

When I broke Babe Ruth's record for consecutive scoreless innings pitched in World Series play in 1961, I joked that maybe I should give batting a try so I could chase some of the Babe's hitting records, too. The truth is, when I look back at the many great Yankees teams that have accumulated a record 27 world championships since the days Ruth switched from pitching to hitting home runs, I realize how fortunate I was to have been on the mound for my hometown team—the greatest franchise in the history of sports.

I was born two weeks after Ruth, Gehrig, and the Yankees won the 1928 World Series. I grew up in Queens and played stickball in the streets, and the great Joe DiMaggio was my early baseball hero. By the time I reached the majors in 1950, the Yankees had won the World Series nine times during my lifetime. That's more championships than most teams have won in their history.

I pitched for 11 American League pennant winners and six world championship teams during my 16 years with the Yankees. I was just 21 years old when I had the chance to start the deciding game of our four-game sweep of the Phillies in 1950. Casey Stengel took me out of the game with one out to go in my very first World Series game and brought Allie Reynolds in for the save—a decision that earned Casey some boos from our fans but one that I understood.

I wound up starting 22 World Series games and winning 10. That win total, along with my 146 innings and 94 strikeouts, are still all-time World Series records. It was a credit to my many fine teammates and the franchise's great commitment to winning not just ballgames but championships. I have been asked many times to name my favorite World Series moment. I have a difficult time choosing just one that stands out. That's one of the great things about a book like this.

If you're a Yankees fan, you don't have to pick one single World Series moment. You have many to choose from, beginning with the first trips in 1921 and '22 or the first championship in '23. There were four straight championships during the '30s and five in a row in the '40s and '50s. Players like Mariano Rivera and Derek Jeter have made sure that the winning tradition has been carried on.

When it comes right down to it, I'd like to be remembered for being a good man, having a good family life, and being well liked and respected by my fellow players. But being out there on the mound in the World Series and winning championships with the Yankees—those are moments I will never forget. I hope reading this book brings back a lifetime of Yankees World Series memories for you, too.

Babe and Claire Ruth
with Yankees owner
Jacob Ruppert

THE MAKINGS OF A DYNASTY

When the tsunami known as Babe Ruth thundered into New York City in 1920, the event marked a sea change in American sports—one that is still being felt nine decades later. With his gargantuan home runs and larger-than-life persona, the Babe transformed the New York Yankees from chumps to champs. Forty times since then, the Bronx Bombers have appeared in the World Series, winning, incredibly, 27 world titles. The St. Louis Cardinals, with 10 championships, come closest.

Just about the time Ruth arrived, New York surpassed London as the most populated city in the world. So with the Babe came the fans. In Ruth's first Yankees season, the team drew nearly 1.3 million folks, becoming the first club ever to top the million mark and setting an attendance record that wouldn't be broken until 1946 (when more than 2.2 million New Yorkers packed Yankee Stadium to see their boys). With the fans came the dollars.

Smart management was always a key factor in Yankees success. Team owners used their riches to build the farm system, acquire needed players to fill holes, sign bonus babies, and (later) to bring the highest-paid free agents on board. Thanks to such Hall of Fame executives as Jacob Ruppert (owner, 1915-39), Ed Barrow (general manager, 1921-44), and George Weiss (GM, 1948-60), the Yankees weren't just a very good baseball team; they were a juggernaut.

In *Yankee Classics,* you'll relive the events that staggered and stunned the baseball world, from the Babe's "called shot" to how the horrors of 9/11 helped shape the Yankees' 2001 near-championship campaign. With the team's numerous trips to the postseason, Yankees who experienced heartbreaking failures have had the chance to redeem themselves. Don Larsen bounced back from a bad outing to author a perfect game in the 1956 World Series. And Ralph Terry, who gave up Bill Mazeroski's World Series-winning home run in 1960, shut out San Francisco (barely) in Game 7 of the 1962 fall classic.

This book's sidebars focus on the legendary sluggers: the Babe, the Iron Horse, Joltin' Joe, Yogi, Mickey, Reggie, Derek, and A-Rod. The tales are told of the fireballers and crafty lefties who made the mound their own personal turf—Whitey Ford, Joe Page, and Mariano Rivera. You'll learn about the managers who helped build the championship teams: "Pushbutton" Joe McCarthy; clown-turned-genius Casey Stengel; feisty Billy Martin, who seemed to spend more time battling his boss than his opponents; and Joe Torre, the intense corporate disciplinarian.

You undoubtedly have seen some of the Yankees' World Series, and you have heard nostalgic tales of their other championship runs. Now it is time to relive every fall classic in which they have played. Sit back and enjoy the show.

GIANTS STILL KINGS OF NEW YORK

1921: NY Giants 5, NY Yankees 3

Not that it needed any extra promotion or hype, but the 1921 World Series was the ultimate Battle of New York, the tenant vs. the landlord. And it all took place in the bathtub-shaped Polo Grounds, the longstanding home of the famously combative John McGraw and his New York Giants, who shared it with the up-and-coming Yankees, who were essentially a one-man show in Babe Ruth.

The intensely competitive McGraw felt threatened by his upstart tenants, in fan appeal and on the field. The Yankees significantly outdrew the Giants at the gate thanks to the home run exploits of their legend-in-the-making, who was single-handedly extinguishing the Dead Ball Era.

It wasn't long until McGraw wanted the Yankees out of there, and the Yanks were only too glad to oblige. Two months before the 1921 season began, Yankees owner Jacob Ruppert announced that the team had purchased a 10-

acre, boulder-strewn lot in the west Bronx, right across the Harlem River from the Polo Grounds. They would build their own baseball palace, a resplendent setting to showcase Ruth's exploits.

But that was a couple of years away. Powered by Ruth, their 26-year-old slugger extraordinaire with an incredible .378 batting average and unheard-of 59 home runs, the Yankees won their first pennant ever in 1921. If the World Series was a bonanza for New York fans, it was a vendetta for McGraw, who abhorred the brainless, longball changes coming into baseball. He hated Ruth, despised the Yankees, and had no use for the American League, even refusing to play the 1904 World Series.

Moreover, McGraw had lost in his last four World Series appearances. Now in the first fall classic played entirely in one ballpark—the Giants and Yankees alternated as home teams—he wasn't terribly fazed that the Yankees were

Elmer Miller leads off Game 1 of the 1921 series with a base hit. He later came around to score on Babe Ruth's RBI single for the first World Series run in Yankees history.

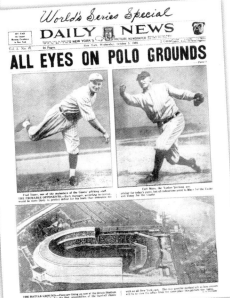

favored to win. But he was enraged that the Bombers were the fans' favorites—in *his* ballpark!

While the Yankees had the firepower, the Giants weren't a shabby run-producing outfit themselves. The team was vastly different than the last Giants squad to win a pennant, in 1917. This club had four future Hall of Famers—Frankie Frisch, Ross Youngs, Dave Bancroft, and George Kelly—and a couple of colorful outfielders in Casey Stengel and Irish Meusel.

Despite the mastery of Yankees pitcher Waite Hoyt—who did not allow an earned run in 27 innings in the series—McGraw's troops hung tough in the best-of-nine affair. They lost the first two games and fell behind 4-0 in Game 3. But they roared back

to win 13-5, then evened the series two days later. And it didn't hurt that Ruth's swollen elbow rendered him useless after Game 4.

The Giants closed out the series with 8-5, 2-1, and 1-0 victories, capturing the all-New York, all-Polo Gounds battle in eight games.

Above left: The Yankees were unable to turn their first-ever pennant into a World Series title. Despite winning four more games than the Giants during the season, the Yanks succumbed to a 71-hit attack from their opponent.

Above right: All eyes were, indeed, on the Polo Grounds in a World Series that pitted the landlord New York Giants against the tenant New York Yankees.

1921 World Series

Game 1			
NYY	100 011 000	3 7 0
NYG	000 000 000	0 5 0

Game 2			
NYY	000 000 000	0 2 3
NYG	000 100 02x	3 3 0

Game 3			
NYY	004 000 010	5 8 0
NYG	004 000 81x	13 20 0

Game 4			
NYY	000 000 031	4 9 1
NYG	000 010 001	2 7 1

Game 5			
NYY	001 200 000	3 6 1
NYG	100 000 000	1 10 1

Game 6			
NYY	030 401 000	8 13 0
NYG	320 000 000	5 7 2

Game 7			
NYY	010 000 000	1 8 1
NYG	000 100 10x	2 6 0

Game 8			
NYY	100 000 000	1 6 0
NYG	000 000 000	0 4 1

THE BAMBINO MAKES HIS MARK

The term *larger than life* seems to have been invented to describe Babe Ruth. For not only was he an athlete of astonishing prowess, he was a true American character almost too big to comprehend. It is said that during World War II, when the Japanese and American troops got close enough to shout at each other, the Yanks hollered, "To hell with the emperor!" The Japanese replied, "To hell with Babe Ruth!"

Ruth arrived in the nation's liveliest city at the beginning of the Roaring '20s and took the town by storm. He was the man who made the home run front-page news. In 1920, his first year with the Yankees after being traded from the Boston Red Sox, he became the first big-leaguer to sock 30 home runs—and finished the season with 54. In 1927, he walloped 60. When he socked his 700th home run in 1934, only two others had hit more than 300.

Besides posting the highest slugging average in history (.690), the Babe ranks 10th all time with a .342 average, including a .393 mark in 1923. As a left-handed pitcher, primarily with the Red Sox, he went 94-46 with a 2.28 ERA, making him the greatest hitting pitcher and the best pitching hitter of all time.

In fact, in his three World Series with the Red Sox (1915, '16, and '18), he was far more impressive as a pitcher. He went 3-0 with a 0.87 ERA, at one point throwing 29⅔ consecutive scoreless innings (a record that Whitey Ford would break). But as a batter in those three fall classics, he went 1-for-11.

With the Yankees, Ruth came alive at the plate in October. In 1926, he became the first person to belt three homers in one World Series game, a feat he duplicated in 1928. His lifetime postseason hitting stats are as impressive as his regular-season ones. In 41 World Series games, he batted .326 with 15 homers and 33 RBI.

Babe Ruth

GIANTS SLAY THE "BIG MONKEY"

1922: NY Giants 4, NY Yankees 0

Same teams as the '21 World Series. And the same story . . . sort of.

To open the season, Babe Ruth and Bob Meusel sat for six weeks after being suspended for an illegal barnstorming tour following the 1921 World Series. When the sluggers returned, many thought the Yankees would win the pennant handily. It didn't happen. What happened was a ferocious battle with the St. Louis Browns, whose star first baseman, George Sisler, batted .420.

The Yankees prevailed by one game, then found themselves once again playing the Giants, their exceptionally talented Polo Grounds landlords. This year the Giants were even better, with every regular (with the exception of third baseman Heinie Groh) batting over .300.

With the series restored to a best-of-seven format, people wondered: Could the Yankees outhit the Giants? This time McGraw's gang was the favorite, and his counterpart to

Ruth was cleanup hitter Irish Meusel, who had knocked in 132 runs during the season. Meusel, Bob's brother, would have another stellar October with a series-leading seven RBI.

Ruth, meanwhile, was coming off a forgettable season, although he became the highest-paid player in baseball history when he signed for $52,000 in March. The deal also called for Ruth to receive $500 for every home run he hit. Unfortunately for the Babe, he missed nearly a third of the campaign and cracked only 35 home runs, and attendance sagged accordingly. In the World Series, the Bambino was simply awful, batting only .118, with one single, one double, and no home runs.

McGraw famously boasted that he had "the big monkey's number—just pitch him low curves and slow stuff and he falls all over himself."

The big drama in this series was the umpires' decision to suspend Game 2 as a 3-3 tie after 10 innings even though

there was still ample daylight to play. A riot nearly developed in the Polo Grounds as enraged fans demanded the game be played to its conclusion. Commissioner Kenesaw Mountain Landis supported the decision publicly but ripped the umpiring crew in private. He then announced that all revenue for the game would be donated to charity.

Aside from the controversial Game 2, the series was a ho-hummer, with the Giants winning easily. Groh and Frisch tormented the Yankees, combining for a .472 average, and were constantly on base for Irish Meusel. The Giants won in four games (excluding the Game 2 tie), and McGraw was downright gleeful that his team so humiliated his hated rivals, especially the great Ruth.

As Grantland Rice, writing in the *New York Tribune,* colorfully noted, "He finished the championship engagement with the classic mark of .118, the most completely subdued and overpowered star that ever had a coronet hammered from a clammy brow."

Above left: A 5-3 victory in the final game made the Giants the big headline-getters in New York City. With three World Series titles to the Yankees' zero, the Giants were still the kings of New York.

Above right: Babe Ruth (*sliding*) and the Yankees were tagged out quickly by George Kelly (*center*) and the Giants in their second straight all-New York World Series battle. The Giants outhit the Bombers .309 to .203 in the series.

1922 World Series

Game 1		
NYY	000 001 100	2 7 0
NYG	000 000 03x	3 11 3

Game 2		
NYY	300 000 000 0	3 8 1
NYG	100 100 010 0	3 8 0

Game 3		
NYY	000 000 000	0 4 1
NYG	002 000 10x	3 12 1

Game 4		
NYY	000 040 000	4 9 1
NYG	200 000 100	3 8 0

Game 5		
NYY	100 010 100	3 5 0
NYG	020 000 03x	5 10 2

YANKEES SOAR TO FIRST WORLD TITLE

1923: NY Yankees 4, NY Giants 2

Dignitaries galore were among the reported 74,200 fans on hand on April 18, 1923, to watch the Yankees unveil their magnificent $2.5 million showplace, just across the Harlem River from the Polo Grounds. Yankee Stadium would quickly become known as the "House That Ruth Built." The largest ballpark in the country—tailored to accommodate the Bambino with a cozy right-field porch—became a dramatic stage for the great Giants-Yankees rivalry in the 1923 World Series.

Intent on wiping out the stain of losses to the Giants in 1921 and '22, the Yankees had acquired lefty Herb Pennock from the Red Sox, giving them their deepest rotation ever. In fact, about half of the Yankees' roster that series had come from the Red Sox, including the catcher (Wally Schang), shortstop (Deacon Scott), third baseman (Joe Dugan), right fielder (Ruth), and starting pitchers in five of the six games (Waite Hoyt, Pennock twice, Sad Sam Jones, and Joe Bush).

But it was Ruth who was all the rage. The Bambino vowed to bounce back from his dismal '22 campaign, which included a suspension, a dreadful World Series, and a dressing-down by New York City Mayor Jimmy Walker at a postseason dinner for letting down the "dirty-faced kids" who looked up to him.

No question, the Babe had a bull's-eye on his back entering the season. Fan frustration was also fueled by his hefty $52,000 salary at a time when the average wage was well under $10,000. But Ruth had worked out all winter and shed 20 pounds, and in 1923 he batted a career-high .393. He also led the league in numerous offensive categories, including home runs (41) and RBI (131). He stole 17 bases and walked a major league record 170 times—nearly half of them coming intentionally.

Ruth's reformation was also vindication for manager Miller Huggins, who had big trouble disciplining his big

The Giants won Game 1 of the 1923 World Series 5-4 on this inside-the-park home run by Casey Stengel in the top of the ninth. Not only would the Yankees come back to win the series, but Stengel, decades later, would manage the Yanks to seven world championships.

1923 World Series

Game 1

				R	H	E
NYG	004	000	001	5	8	0
NYY	120	000	100	4	12	1

Game 2

				R	H	E
NYY	010	210	000	4	10	0
NYG	010	001	000	2	9	2

Game 3

				R	H	E
NYG	000	000	100	1	4	0
NYY	000	000	000	0	6	1

Game 4

				R	H	E
NYY	061	100	000	8	13	1
NYG	000	000	031	4	13	1

Game 5

				R	H	E
NYG	010	000	000	1	3	2
NYY	340	100	00x	8	14	0

Game 6

				R	H	E
NYY	100	000	050	6	5	0
NYG	100	111	000	4	10	1

star. Ruth, in fact, derisively called his 5'6" boss "The Runt." Yet player and manager struck a sort of uneasy truce. Huggins was willing to accept the Babe's shenanigans, especially since he nearly fashioned a triple crown season.

The World Series got off to a sobering start for the Yankees, with Giants veteran Casey Stengel hitting a ninth-inning, inside-the-park homer (the first World Series homer in Yankee Stadium) to give the Giants a dramatic 5-4 victory. But the Yankees hitters would rattle the Giants pitchers most of the series.

Ruth hit three home runs, walked eight times, and compiled a slugging percentage of 1.000. Ironically, though Yankee Stadium essentially had been constructed for Ruth, all three of his homers were at the Polo Grounds.

The clincher came in Game 6, at the same park that the Yankees had shared with the Giants and called "home" for the previous 10 years. The come-from-behind, 6-4 victory featured Ruth's third home run and second victory by Pennock, giving the Yankees their very first world championship.

"This is the happiest day of my life. Now I have the greatest ballpark and the greatest team!"

—Yankees owner Jacob Ruppert, upon winning the 1923 World Series

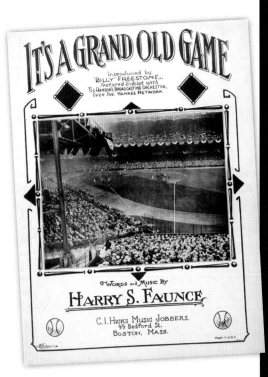

Above: It was a grand old time to be a Yankees fan in 1923, as the team won its third straight pennant and first world championship.

Opposite page: Herb Pennock, part of a deep Yankees rotation, went 2-0 in the World Series to help deliver the club's first championship.

Friction with the landlord—and their two-time World Series opponent, the New York Giants—led to the building of Yankee Stadium. When new acquisition Babe Ruth made the Yankees the first team to surpass a million in attendance in 1920, the Giants no longer wished to share the Polo Grounds as they'd done since 1913.

The Yankees bought 10 acres in the west Bronx from the estate of William Waldorf Astor for $675,000 in February 1921. Owners Jacob Ruppert and Tillinghast L'Hommedieu Huston boldly went forward with plans for a ballpark reminiscent of the coliseums built by the ancient Romans. Completed in only 284 working days and on budget for $2.5 million, the first triple-deckered stadium had room for 70,000 fans and was massive in every way . . . except for a 295-foot porch in right field.

For Ruth, it was love at first swing in the Bronx. The Babe christened the stadium with its first home run, a three-run job against his former club, the Red Sox, in a 4-1 Opening Day win on April 18, 1923. Come October, the Yankees had their way with the Giants, including a crowd-pleasing 8-1 romp in Game 5 at Yankee Stadium.

While the Yankees have won nearly 60 percent of the World Series games they have played in, they have been even better at home, posting a 67-35 record (.657). Their longest World Series home winning streak is 10 games, from Game 6 of the 1996 series through Game 5 in 2001. Surprisingly, the Yankees have clinched the world title on their home turf only 10 times, compared to 17 times on the road.

Yankee Stadium on Opening Day, 1923

RUTH RUNS OUT OF HEROICS

1926: St. Louis 4, New York 3

In 1926, Babe Ruth promised to clean up his act. The Yankees were coming off an awful seventh-place finish in '25, in no small part due to Ruth being sidelined for an alleged bellyache that was actually venereal disease. His eating, boozing, and womanizing seemed to know no bounds.

But just as he did prior to his fabulous 1923 campaign, Ruth came back with a vengeance in 1926. The centerpiece of a rebuilt ballclub, the revitalized 31-year-old slugger hit .372 with a league-leading 47 home runs and 146 RBI.

Overall, the Yankees were a younger team that featured a still-maturing first baseman (Lou Gehrig), a hard-hitting rookie at second (Tony Lazzeri), and a near rookie at shortstop (Mark Koenig). Their pitching staff was solid, bolstered by the acquisition of 19-game winner Urban Shocker from the Browns.

In the World Series, the Yankees faced the St. Louis Cardinals, led by player-manager Rogers Hornsby. Ruth hit a record four home runs in the series—including three in Game 4 at Sportsman's Park. He reached base safely five times in two different games. But the series came down to a Game 7 and one of the most dramatic moments in baseball history.

In a scene befitting a Hollywood script—and indeed, it became the climax of the 1952 movie *The Winning Team* starring Ronald Reagan—aging pitcher Grover Cleveland Alexander was summoned out of the Cardinals' bullpen to quell the Yankees' late-inning rally. Only a day before, Alexander—nearly 40 years old, almost deaf, and subject to frequent seizures—had pitched a complete-game victory to even the series.

Now in the seventh inning of Game 7, with the Cardinals ahead 3-2 and the Yankees having loaded the

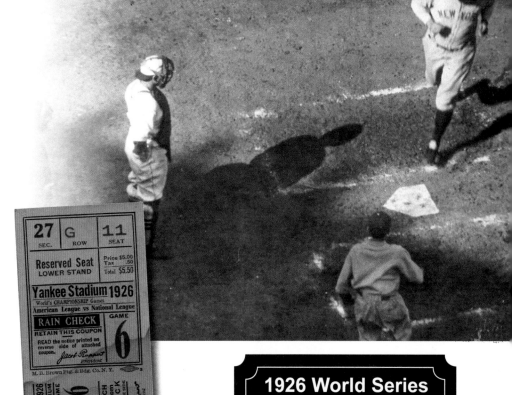

bases, Alexander was called in to face slugger Lazzeri. According to legend, Alexander took a long time to walk in, supposedly hung over from the previous night. Lazzeri ripped a mighty line drive down the left-field line—just foul. Then the old pitcher with the tired right arm came back and struck out the future Hall of Famer on an outside curve.

After retiring the side in the eighth, Alexander got the first two outs of the ninth before walking Ruth, the Babe's 11th free pass of the series. But the Bambino—shockingly and inexplicably—tried to steal second base. He later explained that he was hoping to surprise the Cardinals.

Instead he was thrown out by catcher Bob O'Farrell, ending the series in the strangest fashion imaginable and giving the Cardinals their first world championship. About the only good news for the Babe is that talk radio wasn't yet invented.

Above left: Tickets for the 1926 series were hot sellers in both New York and St. Louis. The first two games at Yankee Stadium drew 60,000-plus patrons.

Above right: Babe Ruth trots across home plate with one of his three Game 4 home runs. Ruth socked four taters in the 1926 World Series while drawing 11 walks, leading to a slugging average of .900 and an OBP of .548.

1926 World Series

Game 1								
STL	100	000	000	1 3 1
NYY	100	001	00x	2 6 0

Game 2								
STL	002	000	301	6 12 1
NYY	020	000	000	2 4 0

Game 3								
NYY	000	000	000	0 5 1
STL	000	310	00x	4 8 0

Game 4								
NYY	101	142	100	10 14 1
STL	100	300	001	5 14 0

Game 5								
NYY	000	001	001	1 3 9 1
STL	000	100	100	0 2 7 1

Game 6								
STL	300	010	501	10 13 2
NYY	000	100	100	2 8 1

Game 7								
STL	000	300	000	3 8 0
NYY	001	001	000	2 8 3

YANKEES CRUSH THE COMPETITION

1927: New York 4, Pittsburgh 0

Do you believe in immortality? Even before the 1927 season was completed, the Yankees—with a lineup referred to as "Murderers' Row"—were being exalted as the greatest team ever. They were simply perfect . . . or as close to perfect as any 110-44 team could be.

The pitching was supreme, the defense without flaw. About the only blemish on this team was so-so catching. So what? The hitting was otherworldly.

Led by the booming bats of Babe Ruth (whose 60 home runs broke his own single-season mark of 59) and Lou Gehrig (league-best 175 RBI), the Yankees had the most devastating 1-2 punch the sport has ever known. The supporting cast wasn't shabby, either. Leadoff man Earle Combs batted .356, and Bob Meusel and Tony Lazzeri each drove in more than 100 runs.

The 1927 Yankees to this day are the standard by which all great teams are measured. The Pittsburgh Pirates were their World Series opponents that year. Also an excellent offensive team, the Pirates' lineup featured three future Hall of Famers—Pie Traynor and Lloyd and Paul Waner, the National League's top hitter with a .380 average.

But there was no high drama in this series, just as there wasn't any drama in the regular season when the Yankees won the pennant by a staggering 19 games. This was your basic October mismatch, or as Ruth later said, "It was over before it got started." He was referring to the longball batting practice exhibition that he and his teammates put on in Forbes Field, which allegedly intimidated some of the Pirates players.

Nonetheless, the Pirates did put up a good fight in the four games. Games 1 and 4 were decided by one run. The hero in the series was not Ruth or Gehrig but shortstop Mark Koenig, who hit .500 and fielded superbly. The pitching star was Herb Pennock, who

Lou Gehrig's mighty bat helped the Yankees make short work of the Pirates. The Iron Horse ripped .308, including two doubles and a pair of triples. Babe Ruth was the only player to homer in the series.

1927 World Series

Game 1

NYY	103 010 000	5 6 1
PIT	101 010 010	4 9 2

Game 2

NYY	003 000 030	6 11 0
PIT	100 000 010	2 7 2

Game 3

PIT	000 000 010	1 3 1
NYY	200 000 60x	8 9 0

Game 4

PIT	100 000 200	3 10 1
NYY	100 020 001	4 12 2

mowed down the first 22 batters he faced in Game 3.

The series sweep returned the Yankees to the baseball mountaintop. All signs pointed to the Bombers entering an era of sustained dominance—a dynasty. There was an aura surrounding the 1927 Yankees, not to mention an unmistakable swagger.

"When we were challenged," said pitcher Waite Hoyt, who had tied for the AL lead with 22 victories and placed second with a 2.63 ERA that season, "when we had to win, we stuck together and played with a fury and determination that could only come from a team spirit. We had a pride in our performance that was very real. It took on the form of snobbery. And I do believe we left a heritage that became a Yankee tradition."

"It was murder. The Yankees had the greatest punch baseball ever knew. We never even worried five or six runs behind. Wham, wham, wham, wham, and wham— no matter who was pitching."

—Babe Ruth, on the 1927 Yankees

Above: Donie Bush's Pittsburgh squad turned out to be no match for Miller Huggins's powerful Yankees. The 1927 Bombers are one of only six major league teams ever to win 110 games.

Below: A 1927 World Series patch marked the Yankees' fifth appearance in seven years. The Pirates, led by Pie Traynor and the Waner brothers, were in the series for the second time in three seasons.

The Yankees' 1927 starting infield (left to right): Lou Gehrig, Tony Lazzeri, Mark Koenig, and Joe Dugan

The 1927 Yankees still leap to the minds of most fans as the greatest team of all time. While that's hard to determine, one fact is certain: those boys from the Bronx dominated their opposition like no team before or since. Take a look.

Their 158 homers were only four shy of the next *three* teams combined. They scored 131 more runs than the next best club. They led the league in every major offensive category except for doubles and stolen bases. (And stealing is a rather dim offensive strategy when Ruth and Gehrig are in the lineup.) Their slugging average of .488 didn't just lead the league, it set an MLB record that still stands. Their average run differential was a stunning 2.4 runs per game. The pitching staff also led the league in ERA.

No wonder they went 110-44 and finished with a 19-game lead over the second-place Athletics.

This was the team for which Babe Ruth slugged 60 homers and Lou Gehrig 47, setting a teammate record that lasted 34 years. Gehrig drove in 175 runs; Babe 164 (first and second in the American

League). Left fielder Bob Meusel and second sacker Tony Lazzeri added 103 and 102, respectively. Three Yanks—Earle Combs, Ruth, and Gehrig—rumbled home more than 136 times each. They were the three top run scorers in the AL.

Even against a fine Pittsburgh Pirates team in the World Series, the Yankees continued to dominate. In a four-game sweep, they outscored the Pirates 23-10. Ruth was relentless, batting .400 with two homers and seven RBI. Shortstop Mark Koenig ripped .500 (9-for-18). Though Lou Gehrig managed only four hits, each went for extra bases.

In the end, some quipped, the Pirates were afraid to pitch to the Yankees. With the score tied in the bottom of the ninth of Game 4, Pittsburgh pitcher Johnny Miljus walked the dangerous Combs on four pitches, allowed a bunt hit, uncorked a wild pitch while facing Ruth, and then decided to intentionally walk the Babe. After striking out Gehrig and Meusel, Miljus threw another wild pitch to Lazzeri, allowing Combs to trot home with the series-winning run.

BABE AND LOU POUND THE CARDS

1928: New York 4, St. Louis 0

The Yankees over the years became so indomitable and inflamed so many passions that Hasbro introduced a board game in the 1960s called Challenge the Yankees. Basically it was the Yankees against baseball's current All-Stars, the implication being that it was difficult for the mighty Yanks to find otherwise worthy opponents.

That wasn't quite so in 1928. Babe Ruth and Lou Gehrig still led the defending champions, but the Philadelphia A's, who boasted future Hall of Famers Mickey Cochrane, Jimmie Foxx, and Al Simmons, posed a ferocious challenge. In fact, they overtook the Yankees in early September and moved into first place. Then the Yankees showed they were, well, the Yankees. They won three straight games over the A's in a climactic series at Yankee Stadium. After that series—which attracted a record 85,265 fans during a Sunday doubleheader—the Yankees recaptured the AL lead, and they subsequently held off the A's for the pennant.

As the Bronx Bombers got ready to face the St. Louis Cardinals in the World Series for the second time in three years, the Redbirds were exuding confidence. If Connie Mack's A's could challenge Murderers' Row, why couldn't they? Besides, the Yankees' cracks had begun to show; they were crippled by injuries to several starters. Ruth was hobbled by a bad leg, and Herb Pennock had a sore arm and couldn't pitch.

The Cardinals felt they had enough pitching, with 21-game winner Bill Sherdel, 20-game winner Jesse Haines, and the still-redoubtable Grover Cleveland Alexander, a 16-game winner at age 41. The St. Louis staff overpowered seven-ninths of the lineup, holding everyone not named Ruth or Gehrig to a .196 batting average. The only problem was the guys named Ruth and Gehrig. They simply annihilated the Cardinals with seven homers and 13 RBI between them. The Yankees outscored the Cardinals 27-10 in

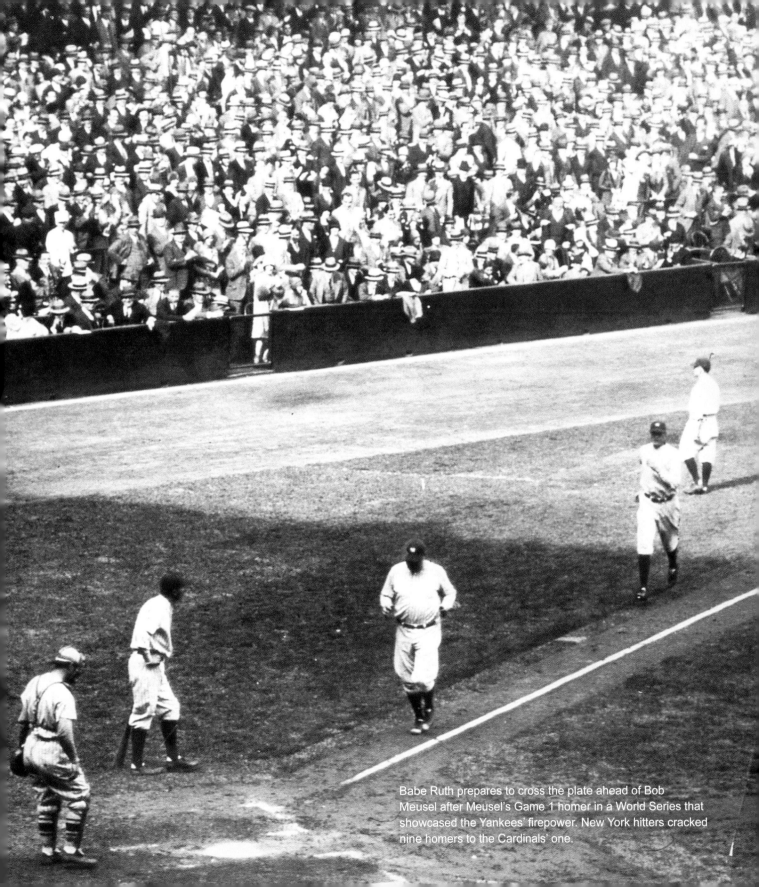

Babe Ruth prepares to cross the plate ahead of Bob Meusel after Meusel's Game 1 homer in a World Series that showcased the Yankees' firepower. New York hitters cracked nine homers to the Cardinals' one.

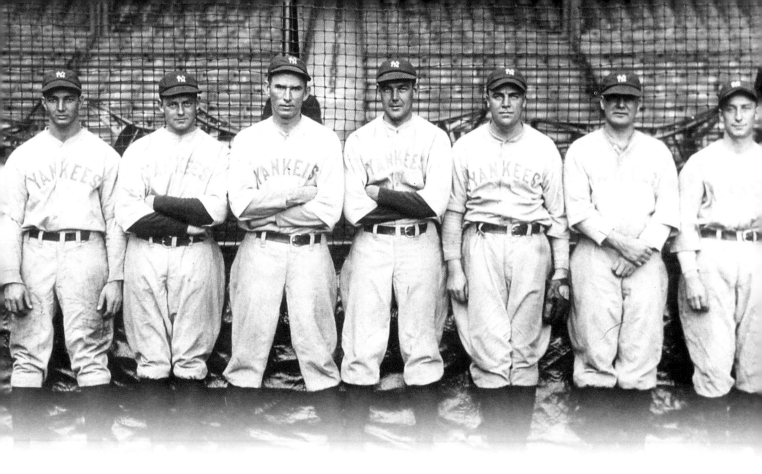

a four-game sweep, gaining a measure of payback for the 1926 defeat.

Ruth batted .625 and blasted three home runs in Game 4. Gehrig wasn't far behind, hitting a blistering .545 and slugging four homers. Almost lost in the Ruth-Gehrig explosion was the stellar pitching of Waite Hoyt (two wins), George Pipgras, and Tom Zachry.

The Yankees won back-to-back world championships for the first time while winning eight straight World Series games. Yet as they savored their second consecutive fall classic sweep, a harsh reality would soon set in. The

1928 World Series would be the last hurrah for Yankees mainstays Mark Koenig, Joe Dugan, and Bob Meusel, who would all lose their jobs within the next year.

Though no one knew it at the time, the 1928 World Series would be the last for Yankees manager Miller Huggins. The following September, he would be diagnosed with erysipelas, and he would die just five days later.

Sure, they were kings of the hill, but the Yankees needed to quickly embark on a rebuilding phase to prepare for more success.

Above: (*From left*) Hank Johnson, Waite Hoyt, Tom Zachary, George Pipgras, Rosy Ryan, Fred Heimach, and Myles Thomas toiled on the Yankees' 1928 pitching staff. Interestingly, the Yanks used only three pitchers in the entire World Series.

1928 World Series

Game 1
STL	000 000 100	1 3 1
NYY	100 200 01x	4 7 0

Game 2
STL	030 000 000	3 4 1
NYY	314 000 10x	9 8 2

Game 3
NYY	010 203 100	7 7 2
STL	200 010 000	3 9 3

Game 4
NYY	000 100 420	7 15 2
STL	001 100 001	3 11 0

Right: A Game 4 rout of the Cardinals completed the Yankees' first back-to-back World Series championships, making them the toast of baseball.

Below: Waite Hoyt, a 23-game winner during the season, pitched two complete-game victories against the Cardinals. He struck out 14 and allowed only three earned runs in the process.

"The Yankees said it with homers. The conventional way is to say it with flowers, but the flowers today were for the Cards. They were funeral wreaths."

—New York sportswriter Richards Vidmer, after Babe Ruth went deep three times in Game 4 to finish the sweep

BOMBERS CLOBBER THE HATED CUBS

1932: New York 4, Chicago 0

As the Great Depression deepened across the country in 1932, baseball attendance sagged noticeably. Nevertheless, the emotions on the field were as strong as ever. A striking example occurred on the Fourth of July at Yankee Stadium, when gentlemanly catcher Bill Dickey broke the jaw of Washington's Carl Reynolds in a one-punch fight following a collision at home plate.

Dickey was one of the Yankees' few holdovers from the previous decade—and one of the key players who would lead the team to greater dominance in the 1930s. Babe Ruth was 37 and slowing, but Lou Gehrig was still productive, hitting .349 with 151 RBI in 1932. On the hill, Lefty Gomez and Red Ruffing became an irrepressible 1-2 punch; they would carry the Yankees the rest of the decade.

In the 1932 World Series, the Yankees had plenty of motivation to beat the Chicago Cubs. New York manager Joe McCarthy had been unceremoniously fired by that team near the end of the 1930 season. Moreover, Cubs shortstop Mark Koenig, a former Yankees mainstay whom the Cubs had acquired in midseason, was voted only a half-share of a World Series bonus, despite his brilliant play for Chicago. The Yankees rightfully felt that their old friend had been slighted.

During the series, insults were exchanged between the dugouts. Fans at Wrigley Field directed their hostilities at Ruth, the most vocal of the Yankees.

After New York won the first two games at home, the stage was set for one of the most mythic moments in the sport's history. As Ruth stepped to the plate at Wrigley in the fifth inning of a tied Game 3, those in the Cubs' dugout started spewing more verbal abuse, calling him fat and old. The taunting prompted Ruth to make a sweeping gesture—what it meant is anybody's guess. Some players and fans insisted that Ruth was calling his shot, while others claimed he was motioning toward the Chicago bench.

With Lou Gehrig (three homers, eight RBI) and Babe Ruth (two homers, six RBI) knocking the cover off the ball, the Cubs were no match for the Yankees in the 1932 World Series.

1932 WORLD SERIES NEW YORK YANKEES vs. CHICAGO CUBS GAME (1) SEPT. 28, 1932 1:15 "WRIGLEY FIELD" (90)

What is indisputable is that Ruth deposited pitcher Charlie Root's next pitch into the center-field bleachers, a towering blast that took the life out of the Cubs. Ruth's homer—forever known as the "called shot"—was followed by a Gehrig home run and an eventual 7-5 Yankees victory.

Ruth snickered as he rounded the bases and basked in all the attention. "That's the first time I ever got the players and the fans going at the same time," he said later. "I never had so much fun in my life."

The "called shot" was indeed a Ruthian moment, one of the most indelible in World Series history. And it overshadowed the Yankees' third World Series sweep, as Ruth's team manhandled the Cubs with 37 runs in the four games. In fact, the Cubs posted an ERA of 9.26, which remains the highest in World Series history. For Burleigh Grimes (23.63 ERA) and his fellow moundsmen, it was a series to forget.

Above left: During trying economic times for the nation, New York Governor and presidential candidate Franklin D. Roosevelt throws out the ceremonial first pitch to get the 1932 World Series started at Yankee Stadium.

Above right: Before the Cubs became baseball's "loveable losers," they were 90-game winners, NL champions, and World Series opponents for the Yankees in 1932.

1932 World Series

Game 1
CHI	200 000 220	6 10 1
NYY	000 305 31.x	12 8 2

Game 2
CHI	101 000 000	2 9 0
NYY	202 010 00x	5 10 1

Game 3
NYY	301 020 001	7 8 1
CHI	102 100 001	5 9 4

Game 4
NYY	102 002 404	13 19 4
CHI	400 001 001	6 9 1

Babe Ruth's "called shot"

One historian called it "one of the largest legends of all time for the largest legend of all time." What Babe Ruth did—or didn't do—in the top of the fifth inning of Game 3 of the 1932 World Series is still debated by baseball historians.

The '32 Yankees were full of swagger. They were making their first World Series appearance since 1928, but they had won that year and the year before in four-game sweeps. The Chicago Cubs had turned their season around late, largely because of the .353 batting of new teammate Mark Koenig, a former Yankee. But the tightfisted Cubs voted Koenig only a one-half World Series share. The Yanks made the Cubs pay in another way, throttling them on the field in Games 1 and 2 in New York.

For Garme 3, Wrigley Field in Chicago was roaring from the benches to the outfield seats. Everybody was screaming at everybody. The score was tied 4-4 when Ruth came to bat to face Charlie Root. Strike one. The Babe saucily held up one finger. After two balls and another strike, the Babe proved again that he knew the count. The Cubs were going bonkers at his audacity.

Ruth was waving his bat around, pointing it toward the Cubs dugout. A film discovered in 1992 seemed to indicate that he pointed it toward the outfield. Root was saying things unsuitable for delicate ears. Ruth replied by sending the next pitch into deep center, the longest home run anyone could remember at Wrigley Field.

For years afterward, the Babe would relish telling the story of how he had announced his home run. He told an interviewer, "That's the first time I ever got the players and the fans going at the same time. I never had so much fun in my whole life." Root's story was different. "If he had tried that," he said, "the next pitch would have been in his ear."

YANKEES' LUMBER
TOO MUCH FOR GIANTS

1936: NY Yankees 4, NY Giants 2

Lou Gehrig was a robust 33 years old in 1936, and he looked like he could continue indefinitely. Finally emerging from Babe Ruth's gargantuan shadow, Gehrig showed he was ready to become baseball's greatest slugger.

In 1936, Gehrig led the majors with 49 homers and a .696 slugging percentage. He batted .354 while playing in all 155 games to keep his consecutive games streak alive. The Iron Horse led the Yankees back to the World Series for the first time in four years. He again shared the spotlight, this time with a slender rookie outfielder by the name of Joe DiMaggio.

The heralded kid from San Francisco quickly settled into Ruth's former spot in the batting order, right in front of Gehrig. He was as shy and aloof as Gehrig, and just as consummate a professional. Later in his career, when he was asked why he always performed at full throttle, he responded, "There may be someone in the park who has never seen me

play before." The driven rookie—who had hit safely in 61 straight games in his first full season in the minors—batted .323 with 29 homers and 125 RBI with the Yanks in 1936. He would soon redefine the art of playing center field.

The Yankees cruised to the AL pennant, winning 102 games and outdistancing second-place Detroit by 19 ½ games. They clinched on September 9, the earliest in American League history. By the looks of it, the Yankees had a new dynasty in the making.

The 1936 fall classic was a renewal of the Subway Series and a memorable matchup of the two league MVPs. Gehrig would go to battle against the Giants' left-handed maestro, Carl Hubbell, who went 26-6 that season and won his last 16 decisions. Nevertheless, the Giants scarcely resembled their great teams of the 1920s. Mel Ott was virtually the team's lone offensive threat. Player-manager Bill Terry was 37, in his final year as a player.

Tony Lazzeri's Game 2 home run was one of seven round-trippers clubbed by the Yankees in the 1936 World Series. New York hammered Giants pitching for a .302 team batting average.

Hubbell got the Giants off to a nice start, ending the Yankees' 12-game World Series winning streak by shutting them down in Game 1. Unfortunately for the Giants, Hubbell could not pitch on zero days rest. In Game 2, the Yankees exploded for an 18-4 slaughter, the most lopsided beating in World Series history. Tony Lazzeri belted a grand slam, and Bill Dickey homered and drove in five.

The Yankees teed off on Giants relievers throughout the series, and the Giants staff wound up with an embarrassing 6.79 ERA. The Bombers brought matters to a close in Game 6 behind the pitching of Lefty Gomez and a well-balanced offensive attack, including three hits by DiMaggio. In the six games, the Yankees batted .302 and scored 43 runs to the Giants' 23.

The Yankees were one year into their greatest four-season stretch in history. A vaunted scouting system had discovered DiMaggio, Gomez, and shortstop Frank Crosetti, all from California. Under the watchful eye of George Weiss, the farm system would continue to harvest top talent. As good as the Yankees were in the 1920s, they became fabulously invincible in the late 1930s.

"It'd be a dream to pitch for a club like the Yankees. . . ."

—Giants ace Carl Hubbell, minutes after the Yankees clinched the 1936 World Series

Above: Giants screwball artist Carl Hubbell was in the midst of an all-time MLB record 24-game winning streak (16 in 1936 and 8 in 1937), but he went 1-1 against the Yankees in the 1936 World Series.

Above: This 1936 World Series program appropriately captures the New York skyline.

Below: Joe McCarthy, far left

Brought aboard to pilot the Yankees in 1931, Joe McCarthy began an amazing string of success when he took the Yanks to a World Series victory in 1932. Over the next dozen years, his team finished first eight times and won seven world titles.

His critics said McCarthy was merely a "pushbutton" manager: Who couldn't win with the talent he had? But McCarthy had his own style, and it began with clearly taking charge and ousting cranky superstars—even Babe Ruth.

McCarthy's career winning percentage of .615 is the highest in major league history. In the 22 full seasons he managed, he never finished in the second division. In fact, he finished fourth or better every year.

In the World Series, McCarthy's teams were nearly invincible. In eight trips with the Yankees, he won seven times, setting a record for a manager that would be tied by Casey Stengel but not yet surpassed. "Marse Joe" (meaning "Master Joe") posted a .698 World Series percentage, a record that has not been equaled. During the 1936-39 "four-peat," McCarthy led his club to 16 wins in 19 games.

BOMBERS DUMP GIANTS AGAIN

1937: NY Yankees 4, NY Giants 1

Good pitching, the saying goes, trumps good hitting. That said, conventional wisdom never had to pitch against the mighty 1937 New York Yankees, whose star-studded lineup struck fear into even the greatest American League pitchers.

Joe DiMaggio hit .346 with 46 home runs and an astounding 167 RBI. Lou Gehrig batted .351 with 159 RBI, while Bill Dickey ripped .332 and knocked in 133. That trio, in the heart of a brutal batting order, powered the Yankees to 102 victories and a 13-game cushion over second-place Detroit.

The Giants, World Series losers to their crosstown rivals in six games the previous fall, won the National League by three games over the Cubs. They hoped 20-game victors Carl Hubbell and rookie Cliff Melton could slow the Yankees bats. Not a chance. The Bombers opened with back-to-back 8-1 routs at Yankee Stadium. Outfielder George "Twinkletoes" Selkirk drove in five runs in the two games, and Hall of Fame hurler Red Ruffing knocked in three during a complete-game victory in Game 2.

Across town at the Polo Grounds, the Giants did not fare much better. Monte Pearson followed Lefty Gomez and Ruffing as the third straight Yankees pitcher to hold the Giants to one run, winning 5-1 in Game 3. Hubbell and the Giants finally broke through with a 7-3 victory in Game 4, with Gehrig blasting what turned out to be the final World Series home run of his Hall of Fame career.

DiMaggio and Myril Hoag homered in Game 5, as the Yankees wrapped up another championship by securing a 4-2 win with Gomez on the mound.

"Pitching, my eye!" yelled a joyous Gomez in the clubhouse after the clinching victory. "How about that hit I got off Melton that drove in the winning run? That's what I call hitting!"

Joe DiMaggio follows the flight of his Game 5 solo home run off Cliff Melton during the 1937 World Series. Joltin' Joe was one of four Yankees to go deep in the set.

1937 World Series

Game 1

NYG	000 010 000	1 6 2
NYY	000 007 01x	8 7 0

Game 2

NYG	100 000 000	1 7 0
NYY	000 024 20x	8 12 0

Game 3

NYY	012 110 000	5 9 0
NYG	000 000 100	1 5 4

Game 4

NYY	101 000 001	3 6 0
NYG	060 000 10x	7 12 3

Game 5

NYY	011 020 000	4 8 0
NYG	002 000 000	2 10 0

Before the series, most considered the Giants a more solid defensive team than the Yankees. But once they took the field, the Giants committed nine errors, while the Yanks became the first club in history to play error-free baseball throughout a World Series. Of course, all the numbers favored the Yankees in this one. They hit .249 with four homers while holding the Giants to a .237 average and one longball. Four different Yankees also legged out triples in the set.

Yankees DiMaggio, Hoag, and Tony Lazzeri each rapped six hits, and Gehrig added five. Gomez won twice with a 1.50 ERA, though it was his Game 5 hit that had the star pitcher screaming.

"You pitched a great game, Lefty, and I'm proud of you," manager Joe McCarthy said after the championship performance. "I'm proud of the whole bunch of you."

Giants manager Bill Terry was critical of the umpiring in this World Series, claiming that the men in blue had failed to see Dickey tipping a Giants bat from behind the plate. He also remarked that perhaps McCarthy should have pitched his ace, Gomez, in the fourth game to facilitate a quicker finish—and put the Giants out of their misery.

Above: Infielders (*from left*) Lou Gehrig, Tony Lazzeri, Frankie Crosetti, Red Rolfe, and Don Heffner were rock-steady as the Yankees played errorless ball in the series. The Giants, meanwhile, erred nine times.

Opposite page, above: A World Series rematch against the Yankees did not go any better for the Giants in 1937 than it did one year earlier. They managed to put just one home run on the program's scoresheet.

Opposite page, below: Hall of Fame pitcher Lefty Gomez was the pitching star of the 1937 World Series, hurling two complete-game wins and notching a salty 1.50 ERA against the Giants. Gomez would finish his career with a 6-0 World Series record.

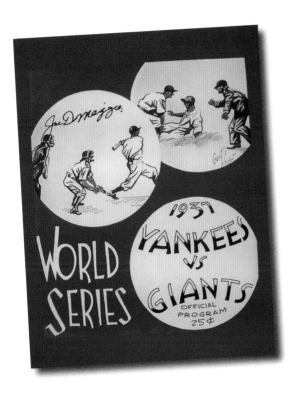

As good as the Yankees had been during the Babe Ruth era, they were unstoppable after he left. From 1936 to 1939, manager Joe McCarthy's Yankees won four straight world championships to become the first team ever to win more than two in a row. During those four years, the Yankees went 409-201 in the regular season and led the league in most runs scored and fewest runs allowed every year. The closest "race" was 9 ½ games in 1938. It was utter domination.

In each of those four years, Red Ruffing won 20 games, Bill Dickey batted over .300 and knocked in 100 runs, Frank Crosetti and Red Rolfe each scored at least 109 runs, and Joe DiMaggio, a rookie in 1936, hit 29 or more homers, knocked in 125, and batted .323 or higher. Lou Gehrig, while continuing his consecutive games streak, drove in 150 runs in both 1936 and 1937, plus 114 in 1938.

The domination continued in October, as the Bombers outscored the opposition 113-52 while losing only 3 times in 19 World Series contests from 1936 to 1939. Twice during the 1936 series they put up double-digit runs against the Giants. In Game 2, sluggers Bill Dickey and Tony Lazzeri combined for 10 RBI, as the team amassed 17 hits and nine walks in an 18-4 rout.

It's Gloamin'
to Gloom for Cubs

1938: New York 4, Chicago 0

It will forever stand as one of the most dramatic home runs in baseball history. Player-manager Gabby Hartnett's "Homer in the Gloamin',," in the bottom of the ninth inning of a September 28, 1938, game against Pittsburgh, lifted the Cubs over the Pirates in both the contest and the National League standings, helping Chicago earn a berth in that year's World Series.

But against the two-time defending champion New York Yankees, the darkness that settled over Wrigley Field and helped immortalize Hartnett's blast seemed light compared to the first week of October.

No team had ever won three consecutive World Series championships. Some, perhaps trying to find a reason to believe the Cubs could compete with the Yankees, speculated that New York might succumb to the pressure of trying to become the first to do so. Manager Joe McCarthy was not among that group.

"The day we clinched the pennant, I said this club was the best I ever managed or ever saw," he said of a team that went 99-53 and ran off with the American League pennant. "I'm still holding to that opinion and so can see only one result. I'm sorry my old friend Gabby Hartnett will have to take it, but we'll be out to clinch this series as quickly as we can."

McCarthy was right. Just as they did when these same teams met in the 1932 World Series, the Yankees needed the minimum four games to assert their dominance.

Tickets for the opening game at Wrigley Field were being scalped for as much as $50. Red Ruffing started for the Yankees and allowed nine hits but just one run in a 3-1 victory. The following day, Joe DiMaggio and Frankie Crosetti homered for the Yankees in Lefty Gomez's 6-3 win, and Chicago fans were beginning to resign themselves to the likelihood that it was the last time they would see their team that season.

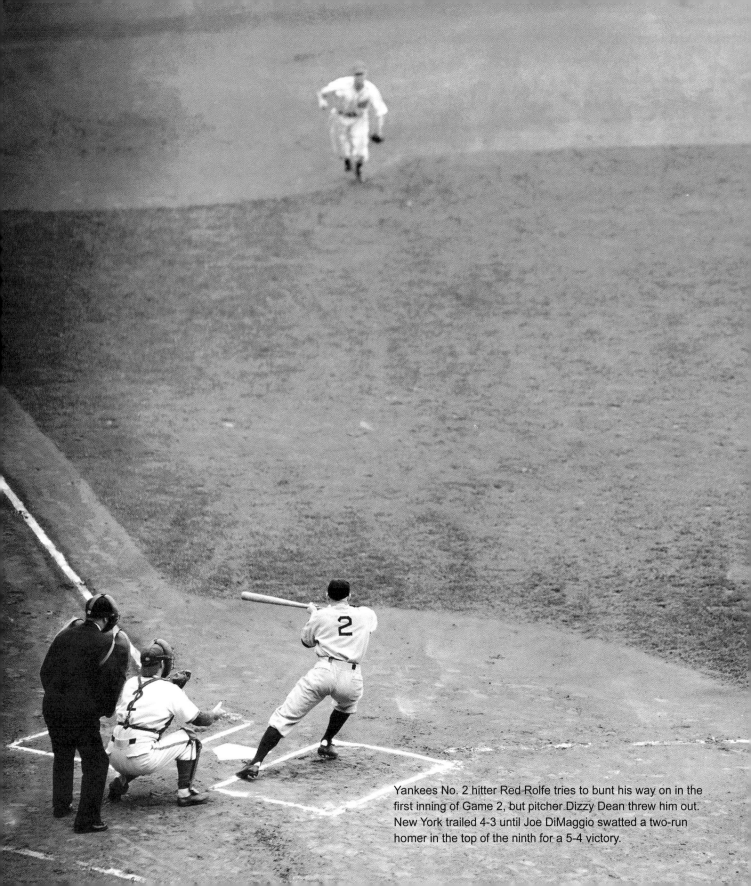

Yankees No. 2 hitter Red Rolfe tries to bunt his way on in the first inning of Game 2, but pitcher Dizzy Dean threw him out. New York trailed 4-3 until Joe DiMaggio swatted a two-run homer in the top of the ninth for a 5-4 victory.

Left: Joe Gordon tied for the Yankees lead in the series with six hits (including two doubles and a homer) and six RBI in their handling of the overmatched Cubs.

Above: The 1930s were lean economic times in the United States, but tickets were always in demand with the Yankees and Cubs playing in the World Series. This ticket is to the series-clinching game.

Sluggers Bill Dickey and Joe Gordon homered for New York in Monte Pearson's 5-2 triumph at Yankee Stadium in Game 3, and the clincher was an 8-3 Ruffing victory that made the New Yorkers the first three-time defending World Series champion in history.

When the Cubs had returned home from winning the pennant in St. Louis to prepare for the World Series opener, the Cubs were greeted by 300,000 baseball-crazed Chicagoans. When they returned from New York after falling in four games, about 300 were there to cheer them.

"Wait till next year," fans speculated. The Cubs would return to the World Series in 1945, losing to Detroit, but to date have yet to return.

1938 World Series

Game 1

NYY	020 001 000	3 12 1
CHI	001 000 000	1 9 1

Game 2

NYY	020 000 022	6 7 2
CHI	102 000 000	3 11 0

Game 3

CHI	000 010 010	2 5 1
NYY	000 022 01x	5 7 2

Game 4

CHI	000 100 020	3 8 1
NYY	030 001 04x	8 11 1

Lou Gehrig

While Lou Gehrig is acknowledged as the greatest first baseman in history, he was overshadowed for much of his career by his larger-than-life teammate, Babe Ruth. And although the duo are forever connected as the most formidable hitting tandem in the history of the game, the two could not have been more different. Where the Babe was brash and bold, Lou was shy and quiet.

As a slugger, Gehrig was an RBI machine, averaging 147 RBI a year over 13 full seasons. Amazingly enough, as historian Bill Curran pointed out, he did it "while batting immediately behind two of history's greatest base-cleaners, Ruth and DiMaggio," although both of those immortals were often on base. Gehrig was no less spectacular in his seven World Series appearances with the Yanks: In 34 games, he knocked home 35 runs. In 1928 and 1932, Gehrig homered seven times in eight games (all eight were Yankees victories). For his World Series career, he batted .361 and slugged .731.

And, of course, he was the "Iron Horse," appearing in 2,130 consecutive games, a record that wasn't broken for 56 years. But by 1938, his strength was diminishing. It was only the second year since his first full Yankees season that he didn't lead the league in any batting category. In the 1938 World Series, he batted .286 but with no extra-base hits or RBI. He was unusually reserved throughout the series. After the Game 2 win, he sat by himself in the corner of the clubhouse, smoking a cigarette, "enjoying it all," he said. Perhaps he sensed that it would be his last World Series.

Gehrig started the first eight games of the 1939 campaign, but his physical ails were painfully obvious to everyone, and he took the lineup card to home plate on May 2 with his name absent from it. He never played again. That July, the team held a day of recognition for him, and the bashful Gehrig gave his now-famous speech. When he said, "Today I consider myself the luckiest man on the face of the earth," he was referring to the people in his life and the "kindness and encouragement from you fans."

Gehrig died less than two years later.

YANKEES ROUT THE REDS

1939: New York 4, Cincinnati 0

For the first time since 1923, the Yankees entered postseason play without their "Iron Horse," Lou Gehrig. Earlier in the 1939 season, an ill and weakened Gehrig was forced to make a heart-wrenching retirement speech due to a battle with ALS, a fatal disease.

It had been even longer since Cincinnati reached the World Series. The Reds' last appearance, in fact, was their "Black Sox Scandal" victory in 1919. Just two years before their second fall classic, in 1937, the Reds had finished dead last in the National League.

Although it was the upstart Reds against the three-time defending champion Yankees, Cincinnati stood to compete thanks to the top of its pitching rotation. Bucky Walters led the majors with 27 victories, and Paul Derringer was second with 25. In a series that required just four wins, the Reds seemed to have as much of a chance as anyone to dethrone the champs. As it turned out, Cincinnati could

not handle a Yankees team that had won 106 games and outscored opponents by more than 400 runs.

World Series veteran Red Ruffing opposed Derringer in the opener at Yankee Stadium, and the two pitchers took a 1-1 draw into the ninth inning. That's when Yankees outfielder Charlie Keller cracked a triple and scored the winning run on Bill Dickey's game-ending single.

It was Walters's turn to face the Yankees the following day, and he ran into an even tougher pitching matchup. Monte Pearson held the Reds without a hit until the eighth inning, finishing with a 4-0, two-hit victory. Babe Dahlgren, who had the distinction of replacing Gehrig at first base in May, doubled and homered in the triumph.

With Cincinnati's dynamic duo already used up entering Game 3 at Crosley Field, the Reds knew they would need their bats to get back in the series. They did rap 10 hits against the Yankees, but all were singles. Meanwhile, all

Without Lou Gehrig in uniform for the first time since 1923, it was Joe DiMaggio providing big-game heroics in a dominant World Series performance by the Yankees. Here he tallies one of the two runs he scored in the Game 4 finale.

but one of New York's five hits left the playing field. Keller, who would soon earn the nickname "King Kong" for his slugging feats, smashed two homers and Dickey and Joe DiMaggio socked one each in a 7-3 win.

If the series' outcome seemed fully decided, at least some drama remained in a wild Game 4. It was a scoreless game in the seventh, when Keller and Dickey homered for a 2-0 Yankees lead. The Reds rallied with three in the bottom of the inning and took a 4-2 lead into the ninth. But shortstop Billy Myers booted a potential double-play ball to keep the Yankees alive, and DiMaggio raced home with the tying run on a subsequent grounder. The 10th inning featured more bumbling. DiMaggio singled home the tie-breaking run, but outfielder Ival Goodman's misplay allowed an insurance run to race home too, in the form of Keller. Then, when Keller collided with catcher Ernie Lombardi and the ball rolled away, no one retrieved it before DiMaggio himself crossed the plate to make it 7-4. The play would be forever known as the "Lombardi Snooze."

After the unprecedented fourth straight World Series win, Yankees skipper Joe McCarthy led his players in singing "East Side, West Side" and the "Beer Barrel Polka." "Don't forget it's nine straight World Series victories, boys," McCarthy reminded reporters.

Above: Pitchers (*from left*) Red Ruffing, Lefty Gomez, and Monte Pearson started the first three games of the Yankees' quick dispatching of the upstart Reds. Pearson, who tossed a two-hit shutout in Game 2, lost his no-hitter with one out in the eighth.

"The way it looks now, the Yankees' complete dominance of the baseball world is not for a month and not for a year, but for always."

—Bill Corum, writing in the *New York Journal-American*

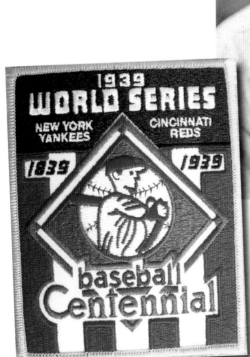

Above: Charlie "King Kong" Keller smashed three home runs during the four-game set, including a pair of two-run homers in New York's 7-3 victory in Game 3.

Left: Just two years after finishing in last place in the National League, the Reds patched together the right pieces to reach the World Series in 1939, a year that was celebrated as baseball's centennial.

A RIVALRY IS BORN

1941: New York 4, Brooklyn 1

Mickey Owen called the Yankees "the real bums," but the Brooklyn catcher wound up eating his words—and regretting a costly miscue—after another World Series championship landed in the Bronx.

Though it did not truly rev up until later in the decade, the Yankees-Dodgers rivalry was born in 1941. Brooklyn captured its first pennant since 1920, and with it came the opportunity to play its mighty crosstown rival. It was a matchup that would become commonplace in mid-20th century World Series play, and it all began here.

While Ted Williams of the Red Sox was pummeling American League pitching to become baseball's first .400 hitter in more than a decade, the Yankees were running away with another pennant. Outfielders Joltin' Joe DiMaggio (who authored his 56-game hitting streak this year), Charlie "King Kong" Keller, and Tommy "The Clutch" Henrich each blasted at least 30 homers for the Bronx Bombers,

who were favored to win a World Series between two 100-victory clubs.

They did just that, in five closely contested games and with a little help from Owen in the turning point of the series.

New York and Brooklyn traded 3-2 decisions at Yankee Stadium, with the Yankees getting an opening victory from Red Ruffing and the Dodgers responding with a Whit Wyatt win. At Ebbets Field in Brooklyn, the Yankees broke a scoreless tie with two runs in the eighth inning for a 2-1 triumph.

The Dodgers appeared poised to tie the series again when, with a 4-3 edge and two outs in the ninth inning of Game 4, Owen mishandled what would have been a game-ending third strike on Henrich. The ball skipped behind the catcher, Henrich raced to first base, and the Yankees proceeded to rally for four two-out runs and an improbable 7-4 gift.

Tiny Bonham (*center*) and the Yankees had a World Series victory and a rivalry to celebrate. The Yanks and Dodgers would become World Series foes 10 more times over the next four decades.

1941 World Series

Game 1

BRK	000	010	100	2	6	0
NYY	010	101	00x	3	6	1

Game 2

BRK	000	021	000	3	6	2
NYY	011	000	000	2	9	1

Game 3

NYY	000	000	020	2	8	0
BRK	000	000	010	1	4	0

Game 4

NYY	100	200	004	7	12	0
BRK	000	220	000	4	9	1

Game 5

NYY	020	010	000	3	6	0
BRK	001	000	000	1	4	1

"Sure, it was my fault," Owen said, fighting back tears after the loss. Ironically, the catcher had handled 476 consecutive chances without an error during the regular season, setting a National League record. "The ball was a low curve that broke down. It hit the edge of my glove and glanced off, but I should have had him out anyway. But who ever said those Yanks were such great sluggers? They're the real bums in this series, with that great reputation of theirs."

So instead of splitting four consecutive one-run games, the Yankees held a 3-1 series lead and had a surge of momentum. In Game 5, Tiny Bonham threw a four-hitter and New York never trailed in a 3-1 deciding victory.

The most dramatic moment came in the fifth inning. After a Henrich homer, Wyatt—known as a headhunter—sent DiMaggio to the dirt with an inside pitch. The Yankees star got up and charged the mound, sending players from both dugouts spilling onto the field. Order was restored, but a rivalry was born.

Above: Catcher Mickey Owen of the Dodgers tags out Joe Gordon at the plate in Game 2. Owen's dropped third strike in Game 4 would prove to be the pivotal moment of the series.

Right: The official program for the 1941 series presented a balanced match-up between the Yankees and Dodgers, although the "Bums" managed only one win.

Tiny Bonham

The World Series exploits of such Yankees greats as Mickey Mantle, Yogi Berra, and Reggie Jackson have been loudly celebrated. But oftentimes the stars of Yankees championships were not Hall of Fame legends, but fill-ins and role players.

Frankie Crosetti was a weak-hitting shortstop, but in 1938 he must have felt like Babe Ruth. With the Yanks down 3-2 in the eighth inning of Game 2, Crosetti smacked a two-run homer off Chicago's Dizzy Dean. In Game 4, he had a pair of two-run extra-base hits to help New York finish the sweep.

Ernest "Tiny" Bonham was a spot starter and occasional reliever for the 1941 Yanks. But given a chance to close out the series with a Game 5 start, he shone brightly, tossing a complete-game four-hitter for the title. Marius Russo had an unhappy 5-10 record with the 1943 Yanks, but when called on to start Game 4, he not only hurled a complete game, allowing no earned runs, but belted two doubles as well.

Billy Martin could pick it at second base, but in the 1953 World Series he proved he could hit. He batted .500 with eight RBI, two triples, and two homers. With Yogi Berra and Mantle injured in Game 5 of the 1961 series against the Reds, Johnny Blanchard and Hector Lopez stepped in and did their best Yogi and Mickey impersonations. Between them, they hit two homers, a double, and a triple as the Yanks ran away with the decisive game 13-5.

Ricky Ledee usually batted ninth for the 1998 Yanks. Yet in Games 1, 2, and 4 of the World Series, he put up nearly identical batting lines: 2-for-3 with a double and an RBI or two as the Yankees swept San Diego. Fill-in second baseman Brian Doyle (.438 in 1978 World Series), backup outfielder Chad Curtis (walk-off homer in 1999 fall classic), and third baseman Scott Brosius (1998 World Series MVP and dramatic 2001 home run) were other Yankees who shined on center stage.

CARDS HOLD THE WINNING HAND

1942: St. Louis 4, New York 1

With World War II dominating the news, New Yorkers could turn to any of their three baseball teams as a distraction, or perhaps watch James Cagney in *Yankee Doodle Dandy* on the silver screen. Once October arrived, their Yankees were anything but dandy on the diamond.

Give the homegrown St. Louis Cardinals most of the credit. No team in baseball finished the regular season with more sizzle. In chasing down the Dodgers for the National League flag, they won 43 of their last 51 contests and went 21-4 in September, winning 106 games for the year. Branch Rickey's prized farm system came to fruition in the likes of sluggers Stan Musial and Enos Slaughter and hurlers Mort Cooper and Johnny Beazley.

Still, when future Hall of Famer Red Ruffing held the Cardinals without a hit into the eighth inning of the World Series opener, it appeared the 103-win Yankees were headed toward a second straight title. St. Louis, however, made a statement that was not to be taken lightly. Trailing 5-0 before breaking through with a hit, the Cardinals staged a rally that set the final score at 7-4. It was still a loss, but one that gave them hope.

Given their propensity for stringing together wins and the unlikelihood they would duplicate their four-error Game 1 performance, the Cards began to like their chances. And it did not take long for those chances to grow into the reality of handing the Yankees their first World Series setback since 1926.

Beazley, a wunderkind who would later ruin his arm playing ball in the Army, took a 3-0 lead into the eighth inning of Game 2 and held on for a 4-3 win at Sportsman's Park. Ernie White then blanked Bronx's Bombers 2-0 when the teams resumed play at Yankee Stadium. When the Cardinals pounced on the Yankees for six runs in the fourth inning of Game 4 and held on in a 9-6 slugfest, it became clear that it was not the Cardinals, but the Yankees, who were in over their heads.

St. Louis won it in five. Beazley earned his second victory of the series, 4-2, with George "Whitey" Kurowski providing a two-run homer. Charlie Keller hit two home runs in the series for the Yankees while Joe DiMaggio hit .333, but neither could prevent the Cardinals from sweeping four straight games after their nearly hitless start.

"There were no heroes on the Cardinals," Kurowski said. "We all played together. That's why we won."

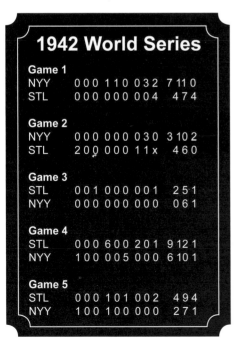

1942 World Series

Game 1
NYY	000 110 032	7	11 0
STL	000 000 004	4	7 4

Game 2
NYY	000 000 030	3	10 2
STL	200 000 11x	4	6 0

Game 3
STL	001 000 001	2	5 1
NYY	000 000 000	0	6 1

Game 4
STL	000 600 201	9	12 1
NYY	100 005 000	6	10 1

Game 5
STL	000 101 002	4	9 4
NYY	100 100 000	2	7 1

Top: Up-and-coming Cardinals rookie Stan Musial slides safely into third base under the tag of Red Rolfe during St. Louis' 4-3 win in Game 2. Down 7-0 in Game 1, the Cards had rallied for four in the ninth before Musial grounded out with the bases loaded to end the game.

Above: With the nation in the midst of war, World Series baseball arrived as a welcome distraction for many Americans, particularly fans of the Yankees and Cardinals.

YANKEES TURN TABLES ON ST. LOUIS

1943: New York 4, St. Louis 1

Nearly a full month before the 1943 World Series, Commissioner Kenesaw Mountain Landis gathered representatives of the Yankees and Cardinals in Chicago and gained agreement on an unusual deal. Due to wartime travel restrictions, the World Series would feature just one venue change. The first three games would be played in New York; the remainder in St. Louis. The Yankees and Cardinals then went out and upheld their ends of the deal, earning pennants over the next few weeks to set up a World Series rematch and spare the commissioner the potential embarrassment of making such an early arrangement.

Calling this a rematch of the Cardinals' five-game victory of 1942 is a misnomer, however. The war had taken its toll on both rosters. Johnny Beazley, Jimmy Brown, Creepy Crespi, Terry Moore, and Enos Slaughter were among those absent from the St. Louis lineup, while the Yankees returned to the World Series without military men Joe DiMaggio, Phil Rizzuto, Red Ruffing, and Buddy Hassett.

Any notion that baseball might take a backseat during wartime was quickly dispelled in those three Yankee Stadium games. Each was attended by more than 68,000 fans, including a record 69,990 for Game 3. The series drew 277,312, breaking the previous year's mark for a five-game set.

The Cardinals committed eight errors in New York but returned home trailing just 2-1 thanks to Mort Cooper's 4-3, complete-game victory in Game 2. Spud Chandler and Hank Borowy won early games for the Yankees, who were expecting better from the Cardinals once the series moved to the Midwest.

"Some of the boys have been unusually jittery," noted Cardinals manager Billy Southworth after Game 3. "I think that once they get back amid their home surroundings at

Yankees skipper Joe McCarthy (*right*) added a seventh World Series title to his résumé. He received considerable help from pitcher Spud Chandler (*left*), who logged complete-game wins in Games 1 and 5 while posting a 0.50 ERA.

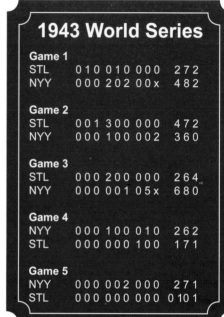

1943 World Series

Game 1			
STL	010 010 000	2 7 2
NYY	000 202 00x	4 8 2

Game 2			
STL	001 300 000	4 7 2
NYY	000 100 002	3 6 0

Game 3			
STL	000 200 000	2 6 4
NYY	000 001 05x	6 8 0

Game 4			
NYY	000 100 010	2 6 2
STL	000 000 100	1 7 1

Game 5			
NYY	000 002 000	2 7 1
STL	000 000 000 0	1 0 1

Above: Bill Dickey's two-run homer accounted for all the runs in Game 5, as the Yankees avenged the previous October's loss to the Cardinals. Dickey would miss the next two seasons to military service.

Sportsman's Park, they will steady down to their regular style of play. If they do, I haven't a doubt we'll quickly even the series and then go on to win."

The Cardinals shored up their defense, but they could not solve New York's pitchers. They managed just one run off Marius Russo in Game 4, falling 2-1, before facing Chandler in Game 5. Chandler, whose .717 career winning percentage is a major league record for pitchers with 100 or more victories, shut out St. Louis to clinch the series. The right-hander scattered 10 hits, all singles.

New York's only runs in the deciding game came on one swing of the bat. Bill Dickey, catching in his eighth World Series, strode to the plate in the sixth inning of a scoreless game with Charlie Keller on base. He hammered a Cooper pitch into the right-field seats for a two-run homer in a 2-0 win.

After the game, Dickey was riding in an elevator with a soldier who bet the Game 5 hero he didn't remember him. Dickey, without missing a beat, identified the man as Joe Gantenbein, a Philadelphia Athletics infielder in 1939 and 1940. "We used to pitch you high and inside," Dickey said. "If we pitched you outside—wham! It was the ballgame."

Such smarts behind the plate, coupled with big-time hits, would earn Dickey enshrinement in the Baseball Hall of Fame.

Above: The Yankees stamped their name on another World Series championship flag in 1943—their 10th in team history.

Below: Joe DiMaggio receives his sergeant stripes. Joltin' Joe served two and a half years in the Army Air Force. He never saw combat, but he was hospitalized due to stomach ulcers.

Twenty-five Yankees, the equivalent of an entire team roster, served in the military at some point during World War II. Some of those players, such as Joe DiMaggio, were on the major league club. Others, such as Yogi Berra and Ralph Houk, were minor leaguers during the war and saw action in Europe before they reached New York.

In 1942, the first year of America's full involvement in the war, Tommy Henrich, Buddy Hassett, and DiMaggio helped the Yankees claim the pennant before departing for military service. With yet more names missing from the roster, the Yankees won a World Series rematch against the Cardinals in 1943. They did so with an obscure journeyman named Tuck Stainback in the outfield. By 1944, even 36-year-old Bill Dickey had left for the military. He had hit .351 in 85 games the previous year.

The Yankees tried old and young to fill the gaps, trotting out Paul Waner, 41, and Johnny Cooney, 43. They got plenty of mileage out of Jim Turner, who at age 41 saved more games than anyone in the AL in '45. But the Yankees' star during the war years was a fellow named Snuffy Stirnweiss.

Declared 4-F (unfit for service) because of ulcers and sinus problems, Stirnweiss became the everyday second baseman after Joe Gordon joined the military. In both 1944 and 1945, Snuffy led the AL in runs, hits, triples, and steals. In 1945, he batted .309, good enough to win the American League batting crown.

YANKS SURVIVE EPIC BATTLE VS. DODGERS

1947: New York 4, Brooklyn 3

The 1947 season began and ended in historic fashion, and in each case the drama unfolded in the boroughs of New York.

Foremost, it was the year the Brooklyn Dodgers broke the modern-era color barrier. Jackie Robinson did it with grace and distinction, stealing a National League-best 29 bases and winning the Major League Rookie of the Year Award. His efforts helped the Dodgers gain what would become a familiar honor come October—the right to face the Yankees in the World Series.

Like the season, the series turned out to be a classic.

"The most exciting World Series I ever saw was 1947," famed sportscaster Red Barber said. "It had so much humanness in it, and it came off of such a human season."

It was the first time the World Series was televised. With TV still in its infancy, the screen rights went for $65,000, much less than for radio rights since very few households had televisions.

While Robinson and the Dodgers made history and held off the Cardinals in the NL pennant race, the powerful Yankees ran away with the American League. Their performance in the first two games of the World Series seemed to justify their status as heavy favorites. A five-run inning in the opener and a four-run frame in Game 2 sparked them to 5-3 and 10-3 victories. There was nothing particularly dramatic about either win.

That changed when the teams suited up at Ebbets Field in Brooklyn. The Dodgers erupted for six runs in the second inning and held off the Yankees 9-8 in a game in which each team bashed 13 hits. One of them was Yogi Berra's seventh-inning home run off Brooklyn's Ralph Branca, the first pinch-hit homer in World Series history.

If that high-scoring contest was a treat, Game 4 was even better—one of the greatest in World Series history. A no-hitter had never been thrown in a World Series

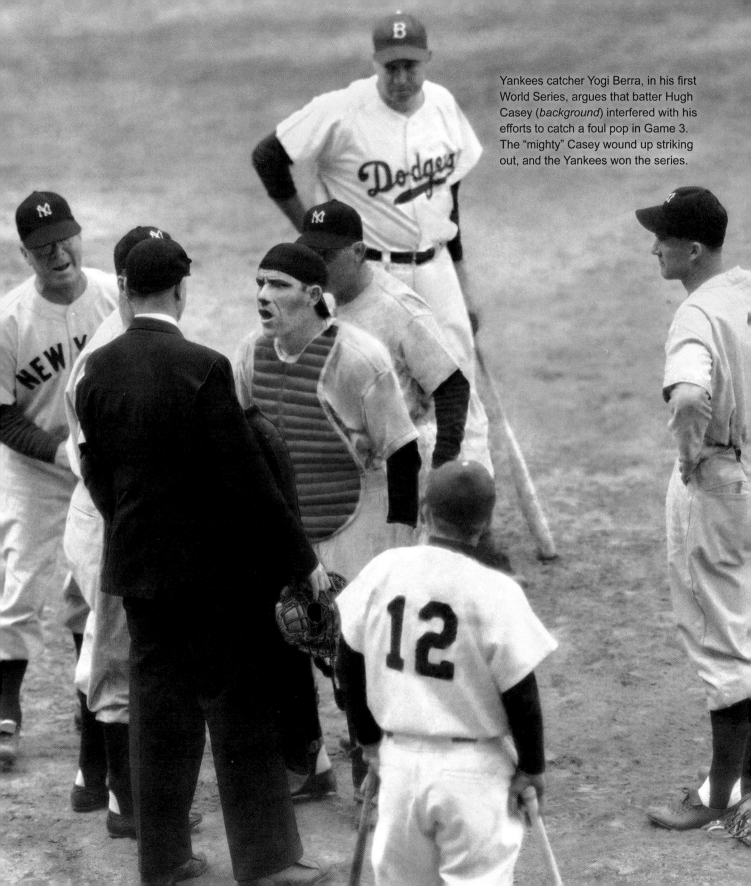

Yankees catcher Yogi Berra, in his first World Series, argues that batter Hugh Casey (*background*) interfered with his efforts to catch a foul pop in Game 3. The "mighty" Casey wound up striking out, and the Yankees won the series.

game, but New York's Bill Bevens was making a strong bid for the first. He was wild, issuing 10 walks, but the Dodgers were struggling to make good contact against the right-hander who had gone just 7-13 during the year. Bevens entered the ninth with a no-hitter and leading 2-1. After a walk to Carl Furillo, Al Gionfriddo entered as a pinch runner and stole second base. With two down—one out away from a no-hit victory—Yankees manager Bucky Harris decided to intentionally walk Pete Reiser. The move defied conventional baseball wisdom in that it put the potential winning run on base.

Reiser became the actual winning run when pinch hitter Cookie Lavagetto broke up the no-hit bid with a double to the opposite-field wall in right field. Dodgers fans spilled out of the stands as Reiser slid across the plate, tying the series.

New York City Mayor William O'Dwyer began taking phone calls almost immediately upon his return

Above left: New York pitcher Bill Bevens bounced back admirably from his blown no-hitter and loss in Game 4. With the championship on the line in Game 7, Bevens took over for starter Spec Shea in the second inning and cooled Brooklyn's bats.

Above right: Skipper Burt Shotton embraces Cookie Lavagetto after the third baseman produced the only Brooklyn hit in Game 4, a pinch-hit double in the ninth that won the game.

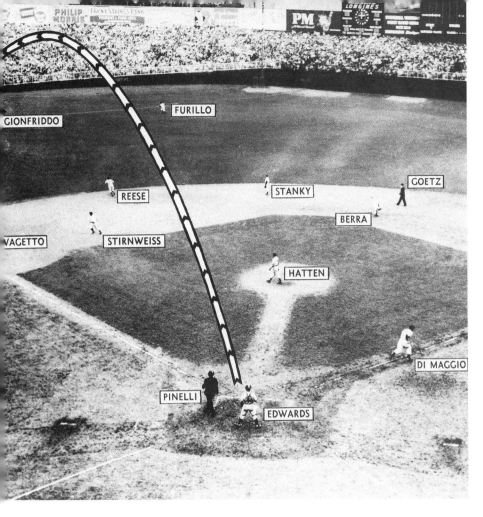

GIONFRIDDO

FURILLO

REESE

STANKY

GOETZ

BERRA

VAGETTO

STIRNWEISS

HATTEN

DI MAGGIO

PINELLI

EDWARDS

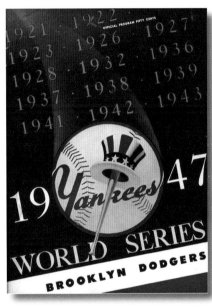

to his office after watching the game. Brooklyn fans were demanding that Lavagetto be named deputy mayor in the aftermath of his big hit. "He deserves anything he wants," O'Dwyer replied, insisting that his own rooting interests remained neutral.

While Lavagetto's hit provided the signature moment of the 1947 World Series, it did not decide the outcome. Game 1 winner Spec Shea helped the Yankees bounce back in Game 5 at Ebbets Field. He held the Dodgers to four hits and drove in the first run in his 2-1 victory. Joe DiMaggio delivered the winning run with a solo homer in the fifth. Shea survived a bases-loaded jam in the seventh.

Brooklyn exploded for eight runs in Game 6 back at Yankee Stadium, and Gionfriddo robbed DiMaggio of a potential tying extra-base hit with a brilliant catch near the 415-foot sign in left field. The Dodgers won this thrilling game 8-6 to set up a winner-take-all Game 7.

Above left: With two on and two out in the sixth inning of Game 6, Brooklyn left fielder Al Gionfriddo made a sensational grab of Joe DiMaggio's long drive to left. The fabled catch preserved Brooklyn's two-run lead.

Above right: A classic World Series deserves a classic program, and this 50-cent souvenir masterpiece certainly fit the bill.

1947 World Series

Game 1

BRK	100 001 100	3 6 0
NYY	000 050 00x	5 4 0

Game 2

BRK	001 100 001	3 9 2
NYY	101 121 40x	10 15 1

Game 3

NYY	002 221 100	8 13 0
BRK	061 200 00x	9 13 1

Game 4

NYY	100 100 000	2 8 1
BRK	000 010 002	3 1 3

Game 5

NYY	000 110 000	2 5 0
BRK	000 001 000	1 4 1

Game 6

BRK	202 004 000	8 12 1
NYY	004 100 001	6 15 2

Game 7

BRK	020 000 000	2 7 0
NYY	010 201 10x	5 7 0

It was a day that would belong to the Yankees. Shea, pitching on light rest, was pulled in the second inning as the Dodgers took a 2-0 lead. But Bevens and winner Joe Page were dominant in relief, and the Yankees cruised to a 5-2 win. Ironically, Lavagetto, Gionfriddo, and Bevens—the fabled heroes of this extraordinary World Series—would never play another major league game.

Above: Dodgers fans turned out in force during the 1947 World Series, hoping this was finally the year their "Bums" might knock off the mighty Yankees. Alas, Brooklyn's supbar hitting (.230 team batting average) doomed their chances.

Managers Casey Stengel and Chuck Dressen

The teams from Brooklyn and the Bronx were the behemoths of baseball from 1947 through 1956. Never has there been a better decade to be a fan of New York baseball. The Yankees missed the World Series only twice during that span. The Dodgers made it six times—and almost eight.

In 1950, the Brooklynites failed to reach the postseason when they had the winning run thrown out at the plate in the bottom of the ninth inning of the season's last game. The next year, they tied with the Giants and lost the three-game playoff on Bobby Thomson's fabled home run. Be it not for these two moments, the Yankees and Dodgers could have met in the fall classic in eight of the ten World Series during this period.

Although they were frequent partners in October, the teams and their fans could not have been more different. The Dodgers, once known as the "Daffiness Boys" because of their on- and off-field antics, were the perennial underdog and played with a fire in their belly, led by Jackie Robinson. In contrast, the Yankees were coolly efficient, almost corporate in tone. Sure, Billy Martin was a scrapper and Yogi Berra was no cover boy, but their overall style was epitomized by DiMaggio and Mantle: quiet excellence.

And the fans? Brooklyn had Hilda Chester, the leather-lunged single mom who had attended the first Ladies' Day at Ebbets Field and was promptly hooked. She carried a cowbell that let everyone in the park understand her sentiments of the moment. She even refused a free offer to sit in the good seats; she belonged in the bleachers. Her counterparts, the Yankees fans, also mirrored their team. They were reserved, respectful, and polite—no roaring Hildas among them.

A New Page in History

1949: New York 4, Brooklyn 1

It was in 1949 that the AL saw its first $100,000 man. Joe DiMaggio became the first in history to earn that staggering sum for a single season, successfully negotiating in February after the Yankees had initially offered their star center fielder $90,000. DiMaggio, as it turned out, played only 76 games that year in support of his paychecks. A scary bout with pneumonia sidelined him for half the season and had Brooklyn positioned as a considerable favorite entering the 1949 World Series.

The Yankees played much of the season with all but two starters still in their 20s, and the young squad famously chased down the Red Sox in the final two days to claim the American League pennant by a single game. DiMaggio had returned for the critical, season-ending series with Boston but left the finale exhausted. With their "Clipper" an ailing shell of himself, if the Yankees were to have a shot against the Dodgers, they were going to have to do it with pitching.

Enter Allie "Superchief" Reynolds (he was part Native American) and Joe Page, one of baseball's first bullpen stars. First-year Yankees manager Casey Stengel handed the ball to Reynolds in Game 1, and the veteran right-hander blanked the Dodgers on two hits in a 1-0 gem. Tommy "Old Reliable" Henrich, who three days earlier had homered in the Yankees' clinching win over Boston, led off the bottom of the ninth inning with a fence-clearing clout off Don Newcombe that sent fans pouring onto the field. New York had a 1-0 series lead.

The Dodgers returned the favor with a 1-0 win of their own in Game 2, with Preacher Roe going the distance at Yankee Stadium. Brooklyn looked to be poised for a championship with the next three games to be played across town at Ebbets Field. Page had other ideas.

The southpaw took over for Tommy Byrne midway through Game 3 and earned the victory when the Yankees

Casey Stengel, who began his major league managerial career in Brooklyn in 1934, celebrates his first World Series championship after skippering the Yankees past his former team in 1949.

1949 World Series

Game 1			
BRK	000 000 000	0 2 0
NYY	000 000 001	1 5 1

Game 2			
BRK	010 000 000	1 7 2
NYY	000 000 000	0 6 1

Game 3			
NYY	001 000 003	4 5 0
BRK	000 100 002	3 5 0

Game 4			
NYY	000 330 000	6 10 0
BRK	000 004 000	4 9 1

Game 5			
NYY	203 113 000	10 11 1
BRK	001 001 400	6 11 2

erupted for three runs in the ninth inning of a 4-3 nail-biter. After a Game 4 win in which New York took a 6-0 lead and held on for a 6-4 triumph, Page was called on again in Game 5.

Starting pitcher Vic Raschi had yielded four seventh-inning runs to Brooklyn, allowing the Dodgers to make a 10-6 game out of what looked to be a Yankees romp. Page smothered all further hopes of a comeback, shutting out Brooklyn the rest of the way. The deciding game was the first in World Series history to be finished under artificial lighting.

In another first, Page became the first reliever ever voted World Series MVP. He earned a win and a

> ## "Not even the Lord could have done a better job with the Yankees than old Casey."
>
> —Dodgers manager Burt Shotton, at the conclusion of the series

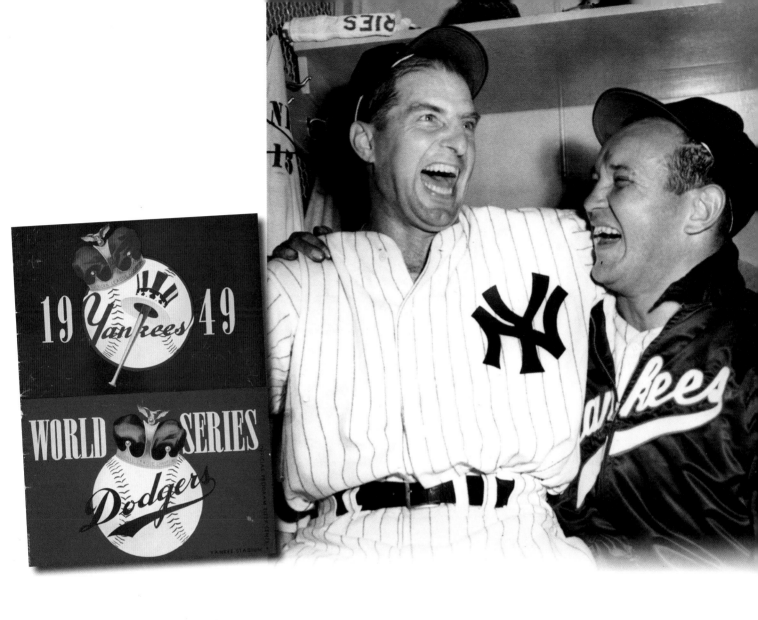

Above left: The Yankees and Dodgers finished the 1949 regular season with identical 97-57 records, setting up yet another World Series showdown.

Above right: A solo home run by Tommy Henrich (*left*) and a two-hit shutout by Allie Reynolds (*right*) were all the Yankees needed to get their title quest started on the right foot in the opener. Reynolds also tossed three-plus innings of no-hit relief in Game 4.

save, compiled a 2.00 ERA in three appearances, and fanned eight batters over nine innings.

Pitching, indeed, made the difference. Against a Brooklyn lineup so potent that big-hitting catcher Roy Campanella batted eighth, Yankees pitchers struck out 38 in five games and registered a 2.80 team ERA. Despite

hitting .226 and managing only two home runs—one by DiMaggio, who hit just .111—New York reigned again.

"I'll say this," said Stengel. "This is the greatest ballclub a man could manage. Certainly the best I've ever known." The Yankees manager could not have predicted the extraordinary success that lay ahead.

YANKS TAKE WHIZ KIDS TO SCHOOL

1950: New York 4, Philadelphia 0

They called the 1950 Philadelphia Phillies the "Whiz Kids" because of their youth and dynamic play. But in that year's World Series, the battle-tested Yankees taught these upstarts a lesson.

En route to 98 wins and a three-game cushion over Detroit, the Bombers boasted the potent duo of Joe DiMaggio and Yogi Berra, who combined for 60 homers and 246 RBI. Meanwhile, the Phillies entered the series with a pitching disadvantage. In edging the Dodgers by two games for their first pennant in 35 years, the Phils had sent ace Robin Roberts to the mound three times in the final five days. As a result, Roberts was unavailable to start Game 1 of the World Series.

Instead, Phillies manager Eddie Sawyer gave reliever Jim Konstanty the ball for his first start of the season. Konstanty was no slouch; in fact, his 16-7 record and 2.66 ERA won him the National League MVP Award. However, it was

an unusual way to begin what would become an unconventional World Series.

Konstanty, like most Phillies pitchers in the set, fared well. He gave up just one run, in the fourth inning, but it was not enough to overcome a two-hitter from Vic Raschi in a 1-0 Yankees victory at Shibe Park.

Roberts got the call the following day and was similarly outdueled on his home mound. Behind fireballer Allie Reynolds and a 10th-inning home run by DiMaggio, the Yankees prevailed 2-1. And so it went for the Phillies, who dropped a third straight one-run game after shortstop Granny Hamner bobbled a routine grounder in the eighth inning of Game 3, which allowed the tying run to score. Jerry Coleman then won it with a single in the bottom of the ninth. *The New York Times* reported that the Phillies' story was beginning to sound like "a worn-out phonograph record with the needle stuck in a rut."

Joe DiMaggio greets Yogi Berra at the plate in Game 4 after Berra's homer—one of only two fence-clearing shots in the series—helped the Yankees put a lid on the Phillies.

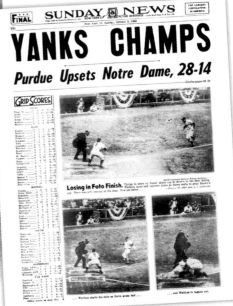

By this series' standards, Game 4 was a blowout. The Yankees scored the game's first five runs in support of Whitey Ford, who was relieved in the ninth inning by starter Allie Reynolds. "The old man [manager Casey Stengel] wasn't fooling around," Ford recalled. "He wanted to end it here and now." Reynolds preserved a 5-2 victory to complete the sweep.

The Yankees won despite batting a measly .222 against the Phillies, and DiMaggio and Berra hit the only two home runs by either club. The Phillies batted .203 and struck out 24 times while drawing just seven walks. New York pitchers registered a 0.73 ERA, allowing just three earned runs. In fact, the Yankees became just the fourth team in major league history to post a sub-1.00 ERA in the World Series.

Above left: Yankees third baseman Bobby Brown scores in the fourth inning of Game 1 for the only run of the game. Brown had led off the inning with a double and moved two bases on deep flyouts by Hank Bauer and Jerry Coleman.

Above right: Catcher Yogi Berra and the Yankees tagged out the Phillies in Game 4 to make front-page World Series headlines, opening a new decade just like they had finished the last.

"Roberts had to get the pitch in the exact spot inside. If it was a speck off, DiMaggio could put it in the seats on you."

—Phillies catcher Andy Seminick, discussing Joltin' Joe's 10th-inning home run in Game 2

1950 World Series

Game 1

NYY	000 100 000			1 5 0
PHI	000 000 000			0 2 1

Game 2

NYY	010 000 000 1	2 10 0
PHI	000 010 000 0	1 7 0

Game 3

PHI	000 001 100	2 10 2
NYY	001 000 011	3 7 0

Game 4

PHI	000 000 002	2 7 1
NYY	200 003 00x	5 8 2

Yogi Berra and Casey Stengel

They were four very different characters, yet they summed up what made the Yankees special throughout the 1940s and '50s. One had a wealth of baseball smarts and savvy, but he disguised it under his uniquely tangled idiom. Another was a prolific Hall of Fame catcher, but he looked and sounded like a New York cab driver. A third was a slick, pint-sized infielder, yet his leadership probably meant as much to the Yankees as his glove. The last was a brash battler who wasn't afraid to use his fists when other techniques failed him.

Casey Stengel was a natural clown, on and off the ballfield. His nine years as a manager in the National League had been dismal, but his five years managing in the minors showed that he knew how to raise a winner. In a dozen years as Yankees manager, he won ten pennants and seven World Series, a string of success no one else has ever approached.

Yogi Berra didn't look like a world-class athlete, but the three-time AL MVP belted 358 career home runs and knocked in 1,430 runs. Of his defense, Stengel said, "He springs on a bunt like it was another dollar."

Except for his 1950 MVP season (.324 average, 125 runs), shortstop Phil "Scooter" Rizzuto's hitting stats were not eye-catching. But his defense was. Said Yankees pitcher Vic Raschi, "My best pitch is anything the batter grounds, lines, or pops up in the direction of Rizzuto." As for his leadership, Joe DiMaggio said that Rizzuto "holds this team together."

Billy Martin's playing career with the Yanks didn't last long, but he was always one of Stengel's favorites. The slender second baseman made a key game- and series-saving catch in 1952 and then earned World Series MVP honors the following year. He went on to fashion a long, turbulent managerial career, which included five separate stints as the Yankees' skipper.

YANKS STEAL THE GIANTS' THUNDER

1951: NY Yankees 4, NY Giants 2

History might recall the 1951 World Series as something of a footnote. The New York Giants had earned a shot at the two-time defending champion Yankees with the "Shot Heard 'Round the World," Bobby Thomson's pennant-clinching home run in a playoff victory over the Brooklyn Dodgers. How could anyone—any team, for that matter—follow one of the most dramatic moments in American sports history?

None could, but it did not stop the Yankees from reveling in a third consecutive championship.

Though the Giants seemed to be a "team of destiny" after Thomson's heroics, destiny proved to be on the side of the Yankees' greatest hero. Joe DiMaggio, at 36, had struggled through his worst year. Playing alongside fleet-footed and strong-armed rookie Mickey Mantle in the outfield, Joltin' Joe was a shadow of his former self, hitting .263 with 12 homers. The 1951 World Series would be his swan song.

The Giants took Game 1 by a 5-1 score at Yankee Stadium. They beat Allie Reynolds, who had thrown two no-hitters during the season. The Yankees bounced back to claim the second game 3-1, but they lost their young superstar in the process. Mantle injured his knee when he snagged one of his cleats in an outfield drain cover while giving way to DiMaggio on a Willie Mays fly ball. The Mick was carried off the field with an injury that would plague him for the rest of his career.

After the Yankees dropped Game 3 by a 6-2 count, Reynolds delivered a strong performance and DiMaggio homered as the Yankees took Game 4 by the same score. Gil McDougald, another talented rookie, hit just the third grand slam in World Series history to help power the Bronx Bombers to a 13-1 rout in Game 5, giving them a chance to wrap up another championship on their home turf.

Former Marine Hank Bauer produced the big plays in the decisive Game 6. His bases-loaded triple snapped a 1-1

The 1951 World Series turned grand for Gil McDougald in Game 5. His grand slam highlighted a 13-1 win, and the Yankees finished off the Giants the next day.

tie in the sixth inning and gave the Yankees the margin they needed to hold off the Giants. Bauer's tumbling, game-ending snare of a Sal Yvars line drive ended the 4-3 thriller.

"Well, the Yankees are still the Yankees," noted manager Casey Stengel. "It's the only club that could beat that Giant outfit three straight. Took some doing, too."

Just as 1951 will forever be remembered for Thomson's "Shot," the last game of that year's World Series was destined to be recalled for DiMaggio's final at-bat. The Yankee Clipper strode to the plate and ripped a double to right-center off Larry Jansen. As some speculated at the time, it closed the book on a career that had

produced nine World Series titles, two batting crowns, and three American League MVP Awards.

"I've played my last game of ball," DiMaggio said at his retirement press conference. Moments later, due to a New York City power outage, the lights in the room went dark.

Above: In the Giants' first game since the "Shot Heard 'Round the World" contest, Monte Irvin played the hero. He cracked four hits and stole home (*pictured*)—the first time that happened in a World Series since 1928.

Right: Meeting for the first time since 1937, the Yankees and Giants had the full attention of the New York sports world in October 1951.

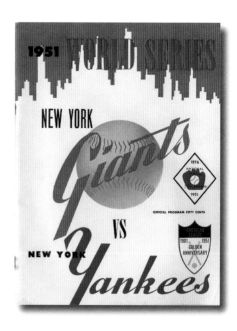

> "I just leaned down at the last instant, stuck out my glove, and got it. I must have slid another few feet on my ass with the ball sticking out of my glove."

—Hank Bauer, recalling his series-ending circus catch

Below: Hank Bauer (*center*) gets smooched by Yankees teammates Phil Rizzuto (*left*) and Yogi Berra after his bases-loaded triple and diving catch won Game 6. In 38 previous World Series at-bats, Bauer had mustered just five total bases.

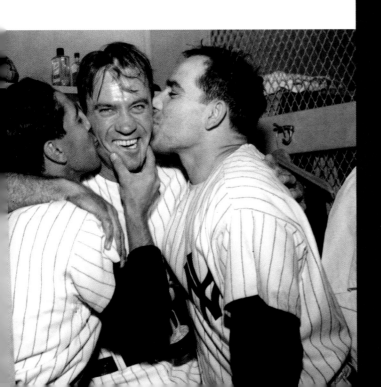

When the New York Yankees (then known as the Highlanders) began play in 1903, they were the poor cousins to John McGraw's NL Giants. Playing in the hastily constructed Hilltop Park in upper Manhattan, the Highlanders attracted only 211,000 fans in their debut season, about one-third what the Giants drew. The Giants were winners; the Highlanders not. Soon, the hapless American Leaguers even became tenants of McGraw's at the Polo Grounds.

When Babe Ruth arrived, the Bronx Bombers improved dramatically. The two teams met in three straight World Series beginning in 1921, with the Giants winning twice before losing in 1923, the year Yankee Stadium opened. The loyalties of New York fans were divided. The Yanks were the team of Wall Street and millionaires; the Giants were the team of the boroughs (except Brooklyn, naturally) and working folks.

The Giants and Yankees squared off two more times during the following decade, with the National Leaguers falling prey to Joe McCarthy's powerhouse squads in 1936 and '37. The Giants then went on a 14-year hiatus from the fall classic, and when they finally returned to the promised land, they were greeted by their old nemeses from the Bronx. Again the Bombers came out on top, giving them an overall 4-2 advantage in head-to-head postseason play.

After the Giants moved to San Francisco in 1958, the rivalry lost some of its luster, but when the West Coast-based Giants made their World Series debut in 1962, they ran up against another formidable Yankees dynasty. It was a classic, seven-game thriller, but the result was the same as the previous four meetings—another Yankees championship.

BOMBERS MAKE IT FOUR IN A ROW

1952: New York 4, Brooklyn 3

It was not for a lack of effort that the Brooklyn Dodgers lost to the Yankees in the World Series for the fourth time in 1952. Duke Snider belted four home runs in the seven-game set, driving in eight runs and hitting .345 along the way. Rookie pitcher Joe Black, who had started only twice during the regular season, made three World Series starts and claimed a complete-game, 4-2 victory in the opener. Pee Wee Reese matched Snider with 10 hits and a .345 batting average while playing superb defense at shortstop.

Yes, the Dodgers had plenty of heroes in the 1952 classic, but so too did the crosstown Yankees, who had won the American League pennant with a 95-59 record. Snider's two-run homer off Allie Reynolds broke a 1-1 tie in Game 1 at Ebbets Field to give Brooklyn the series lead. The following day, it was New York's Billy Martin who homered while Vic Raschi held the Dodgers to three hits in a 7-1 rout.

New York's Johnny Mize then put on a power show at Yankee Stadium. A nine-time All-Star with the Cardinals and Giants, Mize would finish his career with 359 home runs. In Games 3 to 5 of this series, he went deep in each game—and was robbed of what could have been a walk-off homer.

Despite Mize's Game 3 longball, the Dodgers won 5-3 on 11 hits. Reynolds bounced back with a masterful performance to edge Black 2-0 in Game 4, and Snider made winners of the Dodgers in the 11th inning of Game 5 when he drove in his fourth run of a 6-5 thriller. Right fielder Carl Furillo robbed Mize of a home run in the bottom of the 11th with a leaping grab at the wall. The Dodgers' victory put them up three games to two.

Brooklyn was on the precipice, it appeared, of its first championship since 1890, when they were called, somewhat ironically, the Brooklyn Bridegrooms. "I don't know how I feel," Dodgers owner Walter O'Malley said

Mickey Mantle counted four consecutive World Series championships for his powerful Yankees after they took care of the rival Dodgers in a closely contested 1952 tussle. The Mick belted .345 in the series with a pair of home runs.

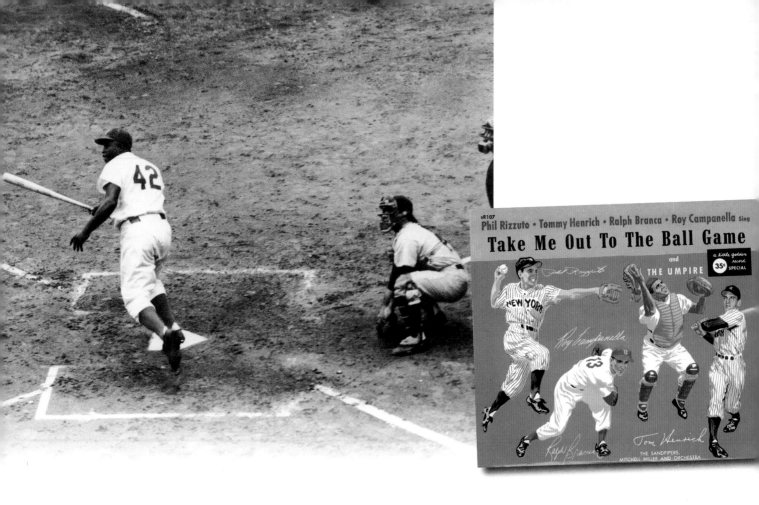

after watching Game 5. "But I think I feel good."

With the final two games set for Ebbets Field, the Dodgers had every reason to feel confident. They felt even better after Snider smashed a solo home run to give Brooklyn a 1-0 lead in the sixth inning of Game 6. Ebbets Field was rocking.

However, Yogi Berra tied it with a homer in the seventh, and then Raschi knocked in the go-ahead run in his own victory. In the eighth, Mickey Mantle socked his first career World Series home run. "I can't describe the feeling when I saw it fall into the seats," Mantle said. All of a sudden, the Yankees owned a 3-1 lead, enough to survive a second Snider longball for a 3-2 decision that forced Game 7.

Brooklyn's Joe Black started against Ed Lopat of the Yankees, although five other pitchers would come out of the pen in this one. Mantle broke a 2-2 tie with a solo homer in the sixth, and his RBI single in the seventh put New York up 4-2. But trouble loomed in the bottom of the inning when the

Above left: Jackie Robinson gets the Dodgers started with a Game 1 home run that helped fuel his club's 4-2 victory at Ebbets Field. The Yankees would counter with 10 home runs during the series, including three by Johnny Mize.

Above right: For this 1952 record, Yankees Phil Rizzuto and Tommy Henrich and Dodgers Ralph Branca and Roy Campanella joined ranks to sing "Take Me Out to the Ball Game."

Above: For those without tickets, New York City watering holes were the next-best venues—particularly those in the Bronx and Brooklyn.

Dodgers loaded the bases. After Casey Stengel called on reliever Bob Kuzava, Jackie Robinson hit a two-out pop-up that first baseman Joe Collins lost in the Brooklyn sky. Just as it appeared that the ball would drop to the ground and that the two Dodgers runners who had already crossed the plate would be marked in the scorebook, Martin saved the day.

The second baseman swooped in to make a running, knee-high catch that preserved the lead, and ultimately, the victory. Kuzava controlled the Dodgers bats the rest of the way for a 4-2 final. It was more heartache for Brooklyn and the fourth straight championship for Stengel, matching Joe McCarthy's feat of the 1930s. Mantle had 10 hits, including the two homers, and a .345 average.

"He's the outstanding player of the series," Stengel said of Mantle, still two weeks shy of his 21st birthday. "And about that record of winning four World Series in a row, it's great to be up there like that, but that's a short record. You have to win eight or nine before you start talking."

"Retire? These are my boys. They never quit on me, and I'll never quit on them."

—Casey Stengel, in the victorious clubhouse after Game 7

Above: Never-say-die second baseman Billy Martin saves the day for the Yankees in the deciding game, making this sensational catch near the mound to quell a bases-loaded Brooklyn threat.

When Mickey Mantle made the Yankees team out of spring training in 1951, everyone knew that the 19-year-old was something special. His manager, the venerable Casey Stengel, said, "He should lead the league in everything." Mantle was a startling combination of raw batting power and sheer running speed. Although he would be plagued by injuries throughout his career, he still played at a level few could match. And, like other Yankees greats before and since, he often gave his best performances on the grandest stage—the World Series.

A bizarre and severe knee injury while running down a Willie Mays fly ball in Game 2 of the 1951 series ended his first season as a Yankee. In his second, he swatted clutch homers in both the sixth and seventh games to overturn the Dodgers' three-games-to-two lead and bring home another world title for the Yanks. Mickey batted .345 for the series.

His collection of World Series batting records is truly amazing. Yogi Berra played in more games and had more at-bats and hits than Mantle, but many of the other career records are Mickey's. His No. 1 rankings include runs, total bases, homers, RBI, and walks. He had five 1.000+ OPS performances, and he tallied at least 14 total bases in each of those series. Interestingly, for the Mick it was often longball or nothing. In 65 World Series games, he managed only six doubles yet left the yard 18 times.

Mickey Mantle

HIGH FIVE FOR MARTIN, YANKEES

1953: New York 4, Brooklyn 2

You could barely watch a play of the 1953 World Series without marveling at Billy Martin. The Yankees' pugnacious second baseman laced a three-run triple in the first inning of the opening game to get his team on the way to an unprecedented fifth consecutive championship. It was his first of three hits in the game and 12 in the series, a record for a six-game fall classic.

It was not just his bat that tortured the Brooklyn Dodgers, either. While Martin hit .500 with a .958 slugging percentage, two home runs, and eight RBI, he also made his presence felt in nonstatistical areas. In a losing Game 4 effort, for example, he gave his team a boost it sorely needed on two plays that did *not* go in his favor.

Brooklyn pitcher Carl Erskine had dominated the Yankees in Game 3, striking out a World Series-record 14 batters—including Mickey Mantle four times—to rescue a club that had lost 9-5 and 4-2 in the first two games. Martin's Game

4 reply? He tried to fool the Dodgers with the old hidden-ball trick, but Brooklyn saw it coming and asked the umpire for time.

Then, in the ninth inning of the 7-3 loss that evened the series at two games apiece, Martin was thrown out at home plate while trying to score on Mantle's single—a faux pas for a team trailing by four runs late. Martin did not blink under the scrutiny of his daring dash.

"I'd try it again if the same play, under similar circumstances, were to come up tomorrow," said Martin, noting that he was given the green light by his third base coach, and that it took a perfect throw from Don Thompson to Roy Campanella to cut him down.

The situation did not arise again, because the Yankees never faced a deficit in either of the final two games.

Mantle hit a third-inning grand slam in Game 5 and Martin also homered in the 11-7 triumph at Ebbets Field, a game that featured 25 hits and six four-baggers. The Yanks

Mickey Mantle belted home runs in Games 2 and 5, both Yankees victories. The Mick slugged a grand slam in Game 5 but struck out four times against Carl Erskine in Game 3.

pounded out 13 more hits in Game 6, a 4-3 home win. Fittingly, it was Martin who strode to the plate and drove in the winning run with a single in the bottom of the ninth inning, sending the Yankees to their record-setting fifth title in a row.

"That Martin must be the best .250 hitter in the world," noted Dodgers pitcher Clem Labine, the Game 6 loser, when told that Billy had hit .257 during the regular season.

"Martin's the best on the club," added Brooklyn manager Chuck Dressen. "He don't try to hit home runs. He just tries to get base hits, and he got 'em in this series."

Top: Second baseman Billy Martin of the Yankees went 12-for-24 with five extra-base hits, including this Game 4 triple, during the 1953 World Series. Martin, in fact, ripped a pair of three-baggers in the game.

Above: Five consecutive World Series championships had a nice ring to it for the New York Yankees of the late 1940s and early 1950s. No major league team has ever matched this incredible feat.

1953 World Series

Game 1

BRK	000 013 100	5	12 2
NYY	400 010 13x	9	12 0

Game 2

BRK	000 200 000	2	9 1
NYY	100 000 12x	4	5 0

Game 3

NYY	000 010 010	2	6 0
BRK	000 011 01x	3	9 0

Game 4

NYY	000 020 001	3	9 0
BRK	300 102 10x	7	12 0

Game 5

NYY	105 000 311	11	11 1
BRK	010 010 041	7	14 1

Game 6

BRK	000 001 002	3	8 3
NYY	210 000 001	4	13 0

"That little Martin is mean. He'll trip you, fight you, or cut you. He'll knock your brains out if he can. He's that kind of a ballplayer. He's the best ballplayer they've got."

—Dodgers manager Chuck Dressen, on World Series MVP Billy Martin

Below: There's room for only one Gil at third base, as the Yanks' Gil McDougald takes a throw from Yogi Berra to force out a sliding Gil Hodges in Game 1. New York erupted for four in the first inning in a 9-5 win.

It was not just the brilliance of manager Casey Stengel, but also that of General Manager George Weiss, that helped the Yankees win world titles from 1949 through 1953. Yogi Berra, Jerry Coleman, Bobby Brown, Hank Bauer, and Gene Woodling, all products of Weiss's farm system, were all 27 or younger in 1949 when the club won the last two games of the year against Boston to grab the pennant.

Led by American League MVP Phil Rizzuto, the 1950 Yankees took over first place from the Tigers on September 16 and never looked back. In 1951 the Yankees boasted rookie Mickey Mantle, Joe DiMaggio in his last season, an MVP in Berra, and Allie Reynolds, who fired two no-hitters that year. The Yanks rallied past Cleveland in mid-September to take the AL flag. The Bombers again won a nip-and-tuck battle with the Indians in 1952. A year later, they won 99 games for a seven-game cushion over the Tribe.

The 1954 Yankees won 103 games, yet they finished eight games behind the 111-win Indians. It was the only time the Yankees missed the World Series in a 10-year span. Now that's dominant.

Dem Bums Get It Done

1955: Brooklyn 4, New York 3

Brooklyn's Dodgers had every reason to expect a long-awaited championship in 1955. They were the most formidable and complete team in baseball. They had seized command of the National League early, winning 22 of their first 24 games. They ran away with the pennant by 13 ½ games, while the American League race went down to the final week.

There was just one problem. The New York Yankees, annual Dodger slayers, stood in their way. And when New York claimed the first two games of a highly anticipated World Series behind the pitching of Whitey Ford and Tommy Byrne and the bat of Joe Collins, who hit two home runs in the opener, Brooklyn fans were thinking "here we go again." After all, the Dodgers had never won a World Series in seven tries, with their previous five loses against the Yankees.

Enter Johnny Podres.

Coming off a lackluster 9-10 slate and facing 17-game winner Bob Turley at Ebbets Field, the left-hander celebrated his 23rd birthday by pitching the Dodgers to an 8-3 triumph that turned the series from a potential runaway into a classic.

Roy Campanella, Gil Hodges, and Duke Snider homered for Brooklyn in an 8-5 win in Game 4, and two more Snider blasts in Game 5 gave the Dodgers a 3-2 series lead heading back to Yankee Stadium. Ford finally quieted the Dodgers in Game 6, recording a 5-1 win, and conventional wisdom held that Podres would be hard-pressed to repeat his heroics under Game 7 pressure.

"Well, the season starts and ends tomorrow," surmised Yankees right fielder Hank Bauer, who hit .429 in the series.

A most memorable season ended with an unforgettable contest—one of the greatest deciding games in World Series history, a classic that gave Brooklyn its only World Series championship.

Johnny Podres, a sub-.500 pitcher during the 1955 season, became the hero of the World Series in which "Dem Bums" became champions at long last. Podres tossed a shutout in the historic Game 7.

"Dem Bums" got another gem from Podres, and this time he shined even brighter. He scattered eight hits and struck out four en route to a shutout. He picked up all the run support he needed when Hodges singled home Campanella in the fourth inning. Hodges drove in another run on a sacrifice fly in the sixth, providing a 2-0 margin against Byrne and the Yanks.

From there, the Dodgers rode Podres's arm and some remarkable defense to a long-awaited Flatbush festival. In the sixth inning, Sandy Amoros, a defensive replacement in left field, made a sprinting catch of a Yogi Berra shot down the left-field line with two men on base and turned it into a double play. Had the ball dropped, the Yankees would have tied the score with the go-ahead run in scoring position with nobody out.

"That was when a penitent Lady Luck," wrote *New York Times* columnist Arthur Daley, "conscience stricken by the many shabby tricks she'd played on the Brooks throughout the years, put wings on the feet of Sandy Amoros and glue in his glove."

There were 18 World Series records set and 11 tied in this crosstown classic, including Phil Rizzuto breaking Joe DiMaggio's mark for most games. The Dodgers were just glad to say goodbye to their old World Series record of 0-7.

Above: Jackie Robinson helps set the tone for the Dodgers in Game 1 with a dazzling straight steal of home against Yogi Berra and the Yankees. Robinson took the risk while his team trailed 6-4 with two outs in the eighth.

"That win meant we finally brought respect to the borough of Brooklyn. Did we celebrate? It never stopped."

—Dodgers pitcher Carl Erskine, after Brooklyn broke an 0-7 drought in the World Series

Below: Slugger Mel Ott said of Yogi Berra: "He seemed to be doing everything wrong, yet everything came out right. He stopped everything behind the plate and hit everything in front of it."

Remembered today more as a master of malapropisms than as the supreme ballplayer he was, Yogi Berra was one of the most important stars of the Stengel-era dynasty. When it comes to career World Series batting records, if Mickey Mantle doesn't hold it, then Berra does.

Yogi was one of the dominant players of his era. He belted 358 home runs, won three AL MVP Awards, finished second or third three other times, and led the Yankees to 10 world titles. He swung at bad balls but rarely struck out, and he frequently came through in the clutch. Paul Richards called him "the toughest man in baseball in the last three innings." Defensively, Casey Stengel said, "he's as quick as a cat."

Berra is the only player to win a World Series ring for each finger—on both hands. His list of fall classic records includes most hits (71), doubles (10), and walks (32). He is second in both runs (41) and RBI (39), trailing Mantle by one in each category. With 12 home runs, he ranks third behind Mantle (18) and Babe Ruth (15). He also bashed the first pinch-hit home run in World Series history, in 1947.

After his playing career ended, Berra moved up to manage the Yankees in 1964. And he did what he had done 14 times before as a player—won the American League pennant.

SWEET PERFECTION

1956: New York 4, Brooklyn 3

In 1956, for the fourth time in five years, the World Series featured two fabled rivals, the New York Yankees against the Brooklyn Dodgers— the Damn Yankees against Dem Bums. The Dodgers, anxious to prove that their 1955 World Series triumph over the Yankees was no fluke, got off to a quick start by winning the first two games of the 1956 fall classic at Ebbets Field.

Brooklyn won the first game of the series behind the pitching of veteran right-hander Sal "The Barber" Maglie, who struck out 10 Yankees and overcame a first-inning, two-run homer by Mickey Mantle to go the distance in a 6-3 win. In the second game, thanks to a grand slam by Yogi Berra, the Yankees built an early 6-0 lead, shelling starter Don Newcombe, winner of the first Cy Young Award after his 27-win season. But the Brooklyn hitters, fighting back with a vengeance, let loose an offensive barrage against New York starter Don Larsen and six other pitchers to win 13-8.

Manager Casey Stengel later admitted his second-inning hook of Larsen might have been too quick. "However," said Stengel, "it might also help to get him really on his toes the next time he starts."

Down two games to none, the Yankees righted the ship when they returned to the Bronx. Whitey Ford pitched nine solid innings and Enos Slaughter smacked a three-run homer in a 5-3 victory in the third game at Yankee Stadium. Tom Sturdivant evened the series at 2-all with a complete-game victory for the Yankees. Mantle, who that season was the AL MVP and triple crown winner after hitting .353 with 52 home runs and 130 RBI, belted another homer in the 6-2 win.

Stengel then called on Larsen to pitch the pivotal fifth game. Brooklyn's Maglie pitched well enough to win most ballgames. He gave up two runs on five hits, one of them a homer by Mantle. But Maglie's performance didn't match Larsen's. Every inning, the Yankees pitcher known as "Gooney

Usually the pitcher jumps into the catcher's arms after a no-hitter, but Yogi Berra couldn't contain his enthusiasm after Don Larsen's perfect gem in Game 5 of the 1956 World Series.

Bird" for his crazy off-field antics retired three hitters in a row. Few Dodgers even came close to reaching base. By the middle of the game, the Yankee Stadium crowd of 64,519 fans woke up to the fact that Larsen might pitch a perfect game. The tension mounted as the game rolled on. "In the seventh inning, I noticed no one on the bench was talking to me," Larsen recalled.

The tension reached its peak in the ninth inning, as the crowd noise fell to a hush and Larsen felt the jitters. After retiring Carl Furillo on a fly to right and Roy Campanella on a grounder to second, Larsen got a called strike three on pinch hitter Dale Mitchell. Catcher Yogi Berra leapt into Larsen's arms to celebrate the only no-hitter and perfect game in World Series history. "It never happened before, and it still hasn't happened since," Berra said decades later.

Above left: Enos Slaughter (*left*) and Whitey Ford celebrate after the former homered and the latter went the distance on the mound in handing the Dodgers a Game 3 loss. Nearly 74,000 fans witnessed the win in person.

Above right: Elston Howard is congratulated by teammate Gil McDougald after Howard's home run contributed to a 9-0 romp by the Bronx Bombers in Game 7.

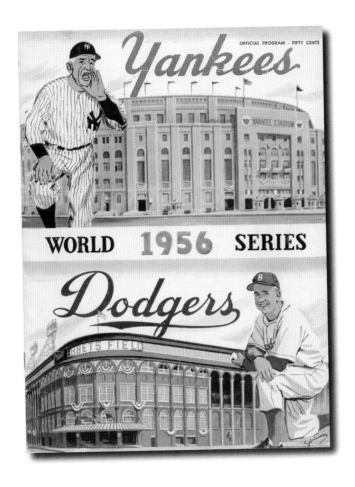

Yankees

WORLD 1956 SERIES

Dodgers

EBBETS FIELD

"I was so nervous, I almost fell down. My legs were rubbery, and my fingers didn't feel like they were on my hand."

—Don Larsen, after Roy Campanella belted a long foul ball with one out in the ninth

Larsen's seven-strikeout, 2-0 gem gave the Yankees a three-games-to-two lead. The journeyman pitcher accomplished one of the most spectacular achievements in baseball history. "Sometimes, I wonder why it happened to me," he said.

The next day, with their backs to the wall, the Dodgers eked out a 1-0 win in 10 innings at Ebbets Field on a game-winning single by Jackie Robinson. The Yankees' Bob Turley allowed just four hits and struck out 11 but was bested by Clem Labine. In the deciding seventh game, Berra hit a pair of two-run home runs, Bill "Moose" Skowron clouted a grand slam, and pitcher Johnny Kucks allowed only three singles in New York's 9-0 rout. The Yankees won their sixth World Series title in eight seasons, a feat that no team has yet to replicate.

The Bronx Bombers, usually noted for their offensive firepower,

Above: Yankees manager Casey Stengel shouts while Dodgers bench general Walter Alston smiles on the cover of this 1956 World Series program.

1956 World Series

Game 1

NYY	200 100 000	3	9	1
BRK	023 100 00x	6	9	0

Game 2

NYY	150 100 001	8	12	2
BRK	061 220 02x	13	12	0

Game 3

BRK	010 001 100	3	8	1
NYY	010 003 01x	5	8	1

Game 4

BRK	000 100 001	2	6	0
NYY	100 201 20x	6	7	2

Game 5

BRK	000 000 000	0	0	0
NYY	000 101 00x	2	5	0

Game 6

NYY	000 000 000 0	0	7	0
BRK	000 000 000 1	1	4	0

Game 7

NYY	202 100 400	9	10	0
BRK	000 000 000	0	3	1

this time relied on pitching to subdue the Dodgers. After using 11 pitchers in the first two games, the Yankees proceeded to get five consecutive complete-game performances from five different pitchers. In the last three games, Larsen, Turley, and Kucks held the Dodgers to just seven hits and one run in 28 innings. It was a total team effort, but the series will forever belong to an imperfect man who pitched a perfect game.

Above: Johnny Kucks lost his hat in the frenzy but got the all-important win in Game 7, setting off a celebration as the Yankees dethroned the Dodgers to return to the top. Kucks, in his only start of the series, fired a three-hit shutout.

When the 24-year-old Don Larsen lost 21 games in 1954 for the Baltimore Orioles, it was a record of futility that only three American League hurlers had surpassed in the previous 22 years. But when Larsen was swapped to the Yankees (along with six other O's for 10 Yankees) that December, things seemed to turn around for the lanky right-hander. He put together a sparkling 9-2 record with a 3.06 ERA in 19 games.

In Larsen's first World Series appearance, in 1955, the Dodgers beat him up, scoring five times in his four innings of work. In spring training in 1956, Larsen drove his car into a telephone pole, and his affection for the grape became known. He had another good season that year, going 11-5 despite battling control issues. Starting Game 2 of the series, he was staked to a 6-0 lead after an inning and a half. But after an infield error and a couple of walks, Don was gone. The Yankees relievers didn't stem the tide and Larsen's log after an inning and two-thirds was four runs allowed. Brooklyn won 13-8.

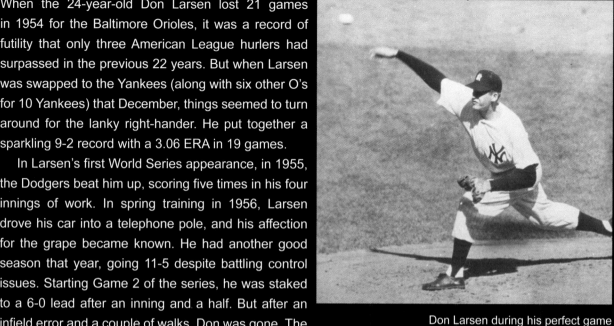

Don Larsen during his perfect game

Three days later, Don had pinpoint control, going to three balls on just one hitter. When he struck out Dale Mitchell looking, with a fastball on the outside corner, Larsen completed the first no-hitter and perfect game in World Series history. It was only the sixth perfect game of all time. Of course, he had plenty of support, including a one-handed running catch by the fleet Mickey Mantle in center. A hard liner by Jackie Robinson off the hands of third baseman Andy Carey was alertly snapped up by shortstop Gil McDougald and turned into an out. Larsen also struck out seven batters.

"It can't be true," he said after the game. "Any minute now I expect the alarm clock to ring and someone to say, 'Okay, Larsen, it's time to get up.'"

Larsen's career lasted 11 more seasons with six different teams. He never again approached the glory of October 8, 1956. But who could?

YANKEES FALL IN HOME OF THE BRAVES

1957: Milwaukee 4, New York 3

Never having played in a World Series before, the Milwaukee Braves would have gladly opposed any American League foe that stood in their way. Their opponent in 1957 was the fabled New York Yankees, who had never before played in Wisconsin and gave the experience a special significance that had the entire state buzzing.

"I'd rather not have won the championship of our league," Braves principal owner Lou Perini went so far as to claim, "if the Yankees hadn't won in the other one. It was the Yankees I wanted our fellows to play. They've won so many World Series that it wouldn't have meant so much to beat any other club."

This World Series, the first for young Braves slugger Henry Aaron, would go the distance, with a Game 7 pitching matchup that had the nation abuzz. One year after pitching the only perfect game in World Series history, Don Larsen took the mound for the Yankees in Game 7. This

time he was merely mortal, as the Braves rode Lew Burdette's arm to a 5-0 win at Yankee Stadium.

Getting to that deciding game required several twists and turns.

The Yankees' Whitey Ford outdueled Warren Spahn in the opener 3-1, but Burdette—who allegedly threw a spitball—pitched the Braves to a 4-2 win in Game 2 before the World Series moved to Milwaukee. The thrill of the event was short-lived for geared-up Braves fans, thanks to a 12-3 Yankees romp in Game 3.

The turning point of the series was painted with shoe polish in Game 4. The Yankees, having taken a 5-4 lead in the top of the 10th inning, were three outs away from a commanding 3-1 lead in games. Leading off the bottom of the 10th, Braves pinch hitter Nippy Jones said he was hit in the foot by a pitch that was called a ball. The umpire checked the ball and, sure enough, a scuff of shoe polish validated the claim. Jones was granted first base. Pinch

The Yankees could not solve Lew Burdette in 1957, as the right-hander won three complete games with a 0.67 ERA to carry Milwaukee in a long and thrilling World Series.

1957 World Series

Game 1

MIL	000	000	100	1 5 0
NYY	000	012	00x	3 9 1

Game 2

MIL	011	200	000	4 8 0
NYY	011	000	000	2 7 2

Game 3

NYY	302	200	500	12 9 0
MIL	010	020	000.	3 8 1

Game 4

NYY	100	000	003	1	5 11 0
MIL	000	400	000	3	7 7 0

Game 5

NYY	000	000	000	0 7 0
MIL	000	001	00x	1 6 1

Game 6

MIL	000	010	100	2 4 0
NYY	002	000	10x	3 7 0

Game 7

MIL	004	000	010	5 9 1
NYY	000	000	000	0 7 3

Left: Left fielder Wes Covington of the Braves robs Gil McDougald with a spectacular catch at the fence in the fourth inning of Game 5 of Milwaukee's World Series triumph. Though no one was on base, it was a pivotal play in the 1-0 Braves victory.

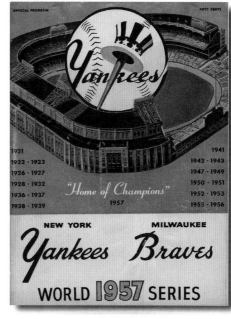

runner Felix Mantilla scored the tying run, just before Eddie Mathews launched a two-run homer to win it.

Burdette edged Ford 1-0 in a Game 5 pitcher's duel to earn his second victory of the series. Thanks to a travel day between that game and the Yankees' 3-2 win in Game 6 at Yankee Stadium, the Braves had the option of sending Burdette back to the mound on three days' rest to oppose Larsen in Game 7. Spahn had been suffering with flu symptoms, and he agreed that staying off the mound was in his team's

best interests. "That Burdette is really one great guy out there," he said.

In the deciding game, Burdette pitched a second consecutive shutout, becoming the tenth pitcher to win three games in a single World Series. He struck out 13 over his three complete games, walked only four, and posted a miniscule ERA of 0.67 against a Yankees team that had led the American League in scoring.

Yankees hitters would gripe that it was Burdette's saliva that did them in, as well as a dab of Nippy Jones's shoe polish.

Above left: Mickey Mantle and a Yankees batboy greet Tony Kubek after one of the Wisconsin native's two home runs during Game 3 at County Stadium. The Yankees cruised in this one, 12-3.

Above right: While the Yankees got top billing on this World Series program, the Braves pulled off the upset, giving the city of Milwaukee its first-ever baseball championship.

TURLEY TAMES THE BRAVES

1958: New York 4, Milwaukee 3

With the Giants having moved to San Francisco and the Dodgers to Los Angeles, 1958 was the first season that New York baseball fans had just one major league team to follow. The Yankees, as usual, made it a memorable one.

In a rematch of their seven-game 1957 loss to Milwaukee, New York became just the second team in history to come back from a 3-1 deficit to win a best-of-seven World Series. (The 1925 Pittsburgh Pirates were the only previous club to do so.)

Yankees infielder Gil McDougald, after wrapping up his fifth World Series title, called it his greatest triumph to date—a thrill surpassed only by the birth of his children. "It was a great comeback for the team," he said.

Manager Casey Stengel, who matched Joe McCarthy with his seventh World Series title as a skipper, said it was improved defense that made the difference. "Go," he told reporters. "Forget about me. Give the boys the credit. They did the job."

Warren Spahn and 1957 World Series hero Lew Burdette led the Braves to victories in the first two games at Milwaukee's County Stadium. The first was a 4-3, 10-inning affair that seemed to take the life out of the Yankees, who then dropped Game 2 by a score of 13-5. Don Larsen shut out the Braves as the set moved to Yankee Stadium, but Spahn returned the favor with a two-hitter in Game 4, putting Milwaukee on the brink of back-to-back titles.

Bob Turley, however, would have none of it.

Coming off a season in which he had won a league-best 21 games and the Major League Cy Young Award, the Game 2 loser blanked the Braves on five hits in Game 5. The hard-throwing right-hander, known as "Bullet Bob," then picked up a save in Game 6, a 10-inning contest that proved to be the key to the championship. McDougald snapped a 2-all tie with a solo homer in the top of the 10th inning, and Bill Skowron added an RBI single. The Braves

Bob Turley (*getting congratulated*) and the Yankees had plenty to celebrate after the 1958 World Series. They reversed their previous year's fortunes against the Braves despite hitting a mere .210 over the seven games.

1958 World Series				
Game 1				
MIL	000	000	100	1 5 0
NYY	000	012	00x	3 9 1
Game 2				
MIL	011	200	000	4 8 0
NYY	011	000	000	2 7 2
Game 3				
NYY	302	200	500	12 9 0
MIL	010	020	000	3 8 1
Game 4				
NYY	100	000	003 1	5 11 0
MIL	000	400	000 3	7 7 0
Game 5				
NYY	000	000	000	0 7 0
MIL	000	001	00x	1 6 1
Game 6				
MIL	000	010	100	2 4 0
NYY	002	000	10x	3 7 0
Game 7				
MIL	004	000	010	5 9 1
NYY	000	000	000	0 7 3

pulled within one in the bottom of the 10th and had the potential tying run on third base, but Turley came on for the final out to earn the save.

Larsen started a Game 7 against Milwaukee for the second straight year, but he encountered early control problems and was given the hook. Turley entered in the third inning with New York up 2-1, and again the Braves couldn't solve him, mustering only two hits and one run over his 6 ⅔ innings of work. The Yankees snapped a 2-2 tie with four runs in the eighth inning and prevailed 6-2.

Turley finished the set with 13 strikeouts, a 2-1 record, one save, and a 2.76 ERA in four games, and he drove off in a new car for being voted MVP.

Above: Hank Aaron of the Braves reaches first base safely despite the Yankees' best efforts on a wild play at County Stadium during the 1958 World Series. The future home run king hit .333 during the series but could not reach the seats.

Right: The Yankees turned their 24th American League flag into an 18th World Series championship, distancing themselves among baseball's elite.

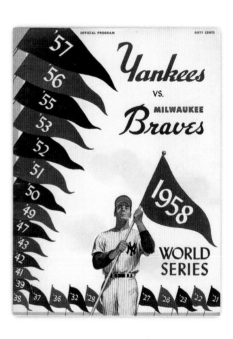

> **"Well, I guess that we showed them we could play in the National League."**
>
> —Casey Stengel, after winning the 1958 World Series (Lew Burdette had quipped a year earlier that the Yankees couldn't finish fifth in the NL)

Below: Bob Turley flexes his muscles in the clubhouse after flexing his pitching might in a Game 7 relief effort that sent the Yankees to victory over the Braves.

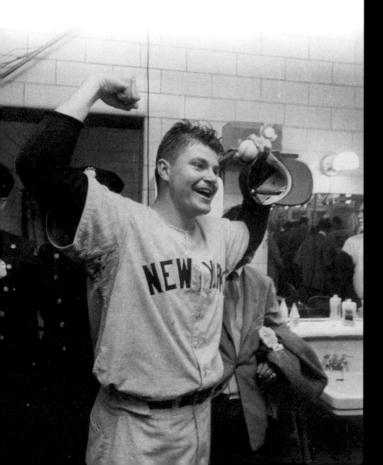

The Yankees in Game 7s of the World Series:

1926, hosting St. Louis: A two-out, ninth-inning baserunning blunder by Babe Ruth ends the game.

1947, hosting Brooklyn: Joe Page's efficient five-inning relief stint wins it for the Yanks.

1952, at Brooklyn: With two outs and the bases loaded in the seventh inning, an infield pop by Jackie Robinson looks like it'll fall in, but Billy Martin charges in to make a shoestring, rally-killing catch.

1955, hosting Brooklyn: A sensational catch by Sandy Amoros and a stalwart pitching effort by Johnny Podres claims the title for Brooklyn.

1956, at Brooklyn: The Yanks return the favor with a Johnny Kucks three-hitter in a 9-0 clincher.

1957, hosting Milwaukee: Former Yankee Lew Burdette's shutout in Game 7 is his third win.

1958, at Milwaukee: This time Bob Turley out-pitches Burdette for a 6-2 finale.

1960, at Pittsburgh: The Pirates win it all when Bill Mazeroski leads off the ninth with a homer.

1962, at San Francisco: Yankee Ralph Terry and Jack Sanford meet in three bristling mound duels; the final is a 1-0 masterpiece by Terry.

1964, at St. Louis: On two days' rest, Cardinals hurler Bob Gibson bests rookie Mel Stottlemyre.

2001, at Arizona: A ninth-inning rally against New York's Mariano Rivera ends with a bloop single over a drawn-in infield by Luis Gonzalez.

HEARTBREAK IN STEEL TOWN

1960: Pittsburgh 4, Yankees 3

Looking at the statistics, the 1960 World Series should have been won by the New York Yankees. The Bronx Bombers set a number of series records, including highest batting average (.338), most hits (91), and most runs (55). But this October, the Yankees lost to the Pittsburgh Pirates, four games to three, on the only Game 7 walk-off home run in World Series history.

The first six games of the 1960 series took on an unusual tone, with the Pirates winning three games by close scores and the Yankees winning three games by a combined 35 runs. After the Pirates won the opener 6-4, the Yankees came back in Games 2 and 3 to pound the Pirates to a pulp, 16-3 and 10-0. Mickey Mantle homered twice in Game 2, and Bobby Richardson drove in a World Series-record six runs in Game 3 on his way to a record 12 RBI for the series.

Pittsburgh tamed New York's bats in winning Games 4 and 5 by scores of 3-2 and 5-2. New York answered in Game 6 by routing the Pirates 12-0 behind Whitey Ford's second shutout of the series.

In the deciding seventh game, New York rolled to a 7-4 lead in the eighth inning. Just six outs separated the Yankees from their 19th title. "I thought that would do it," said Yogi Berra. "We had a lot of good pitchers to hold the lead."

But the Pirates stormed back in the bottom of the eighth inning, scoring five runs. The first key play was a groundball to Tony Kubek that took a bad hop and hit the Yankees shortstop in the throat, allowing the Pittsburgh rally to continue. The next big moment came when Hal Smith socked a three-run homer to put the Pirates up 9-7—a pivotal blow that would soon be lost to history.

In the top of the ninth inning, with the Yankees on the verge of defeat, Mantle singled to knock in one run. He then made a sensational baserunning play to elude a tag while diving back to first base, allowing the tying run to score.

Bill Mazeroski reaches the plate, and his joyous Pirates teammates, after hitting one of the most legendary home runs in baseball history—a Game 7 winner to thwart the Yankees. It is the only walk-off Game 7 home run in World Series history.

That set the stage for Pittsburgh second baseman Bill Mazeroski, the leadoff batter in the bottom of the ninth. Facing Ralph Terry, the fifth Yankees pitcher in the game, Mazeroski took the first pitch for a ball. On the next offering, he blasted a high fly ball that cleared the left-field wall for a home run to win the series for the Pirates.

Mazeroski jumped up and down, waving his cap in the air, like a robot gone wild. There were so many people on the field blocking his way that by the time he rounded third base, he was barely able to touch home plate. He did make it home, though, and the Pirates won 10-9. The home run brought a dramatic conclusion to an improbable series in which the resourceful Pirates had been outhit 91-60 and outscored 55-27.

Afterward in the Yankees clubhouse, the press hounded Terry, the losing pitcher. When asked if he had thrown Mazeroski a fastball or curve, a dejected Terry said, "I don't know what the pitch was. All I know is it was the wrong one."

Above: The Yankees gave pitcher Whitey Ford plenty of backing on the scoreboard in Game 6. Ford won 12-0, setting up a winner-take-all contest at Pittsburgh's Forbes Field.

"All I could think of was how the Yankees used to beat up on Cleveland for years and years, and how the Yankees would come back and how, just now, they'd come back on us with all that hitting. I felt so bad; we all did."

—Native Ohioan Bill Mazeroski, on what he was thinking about before he belted his historic home run

Above right: With the Yankees trailing 9-8 in the top of the ninth of Game 7, Gil McDougald stood on third and Mickey Mantle on first with one out. Yogi Berra grounded to first baseman Rocky Nelson, who stepped on the bag for the second out. Instead of instinctively running to second—where he would have been thrown out—Mantle dove safely back to first (*pictured*), allowing the tying run to score.

Below right: If you like offense, the 1960 World Series was the ticket for you. The winning team scored 10 or more runs in four of the seven games.

REDS LOOK PALE AGAINST WHITEY

1961: New York 4, Cincinnati 1

Babe Ruth was still making headlines in 1961, as home runs were on everyone's mind. The New York Yankees won 109 games and, fueled by Mickey Mantle and Roger Maris—the "M&M Boys"—hit an earth-shaking 240 home runs, a record that would stand for 35 years.

That year, Maris and Mantle both made a run at Ruth's single-season home run record of 60, established in 1927. Mantle started out red-hot, but injuries forced him to drop out of the race in mid-September with 54 homers. Maris pulled ahead and claimed the record with his 61st four-bagger on the last day of the season.

"People always talk about the home run battle as the thing that made us such a great team," said rookie manager Ralph Houk. "It wasn't that. It was our pitching and defense."

Leading the way was Whitey Ford, who had a 25-4 record and received the Cy Young Award for best pitcher at a time when hurlers in both leagues competed for only one award. After Maris surpassed the Babe's season record for home runs, Ford knocked the Bambino out of the World Series record book. As a Boston Red Sox pitcher, the Babe had pitched 29 consecutive scoreless innings in the 1916 and 1918 World Series. Ruth would often say that this was his proudest accomplishment in baseball, greater than any of his batting feats. After twice shutting out Pittsburgh in 1960, Ford continued his mastery against the Cincinnati Reds in the 1961 World Series. The Reds, National League pennant-winners for the first time in 21 years, were no match for the mighty Yanks, who won easily in five games.

Ford started Game 1 at Yankee Stadium and pitched a two-hit shutout. The Reds' only victory came in Game 2 in support of pitcher Joey Jay, the first former Little Leaguer to reach the big leagues. In Game 3 at Cincinnati's Crosley Field, a Roger Maris home run broke a 2-2 tie in the top

Whitey Ford flashes the MVP form he used to dominate the 1961 World Series. The Chairman of the Board went 2-0 while not allowing an earned run in 14 innings.

of the ninth inning, and relief ace Luis Arroyo slithered out of a jam in the bottom of the ninth to preserve the victory. Maris's homer was "the most damaging blow of the series," said Reds manager Fred Hutchinson. "After that we couldn't bounce back."

The Yankees put a stranglehold on the series in Game 4 as Ford and Jim Coates combined on a 7-0 shutout. The Yanks cruised to a 13-5 runaway in the clinching game and celebrated as champions again. Role players took center stage in the series. Second

baseman Bobby Richardson had nine hits, a record for a five-game series; backup catcher Johnny Blanchard hit two home runs; and Hector Lopez, in place of the ailing Mantle, drove in seven runs.

Ford, who was honored with the series MVP Award, won two games and pitched 14 shutout innings to extend his World Series streak to 32 consecutive scoreless frames, breaking the old record held by Ruth. Historian Robert Creamer wryly noted: "It was a bad year for the Babe."

1961 World Series

Game 1
CIN	000 000 000	0 2 0
NYY	000 101 00x	2 6 0

Game 2
CIN	000 211 020	6 9 0
NYY	000 200 000	2 4 3

Game 3
NYY	000 000 111	3 6 1
CIN	001 000 100	2 8 0

Game 4
NYY	000 112 300	7 11 0
CIN	000 000 000	0 5 1

Game 5
NYY	510 502 000	13 15 1
CIN	003 020 000	5 11 3

Opposite page, left: After launching a record 61 home runs during the regular season, Roger Maris went deep once—a ninth-inning game-winner in Game 3—in a five-game World Series win over the Reds.

Opposite page, right: Having succeeded Casey Stengel as manager of the Yankees, Ralph Houk got front-cover program billing for the 1961 World Series.

Below: In the 1961 fall classic, New York's Johnny Blanchard built on a breakout season in which he batted .305. He homered in two World Series games and hit .400 to help the Yankees oust Cincinnati.

After all the stress involved in his pursuit of 61 home runs to break Babe Ruth's record during the 1961 season, the World Series was certainly not stress-free for Roger Maris. Nevertheless, the sullen outfielder came through once again.

The Yankees played the series essentially a man down. Mickey Mantle's virus turned worse when an examination by a doctor led to an infection that knocked him out of his chase of 61 homers; he finished with 54. Mantle played in just two World Series games against Cincinnati, as Maris took over in center field for his friend.

With Game 3 tied in the top of the ninth inning, Maris stepped to the plate hitless in 10 series at-bats. Maris cracked a Bob Purkey offering 20 rows back in right field, and the Yankees won 3-2. New York routed the Reds in the next two games at Crosley Field for the world championship cherry on top of a 109-win season and Maris's record. Maris hit just .105 (2-for-19) against the Reds, but he had the hit that turned the series.

YANKEES DODGE A GIANT BULLET

1962: New York 4, San Francisco 3

In 1962, the New York Yankees clubbed 199 home runs, modest compared to their 1961 super-season but good enough for 96 wins and a World Series appearance for the 12th time in 14 years. Over in the National League, the San Francisco Giants earned their first trip to the World Series (they had relocated from New York in 1958) by brushing off the Los Angeles Dodgers in a grueling three-game playoff series.

The Yankees cruised to a 6-2 victory in Game 1 at San Francisco's Candlestick Park, thanks largely to Clete Boyer's tie-breaking home run. Whitey Ford went all the way for his record 10th World Series victory, though his series-record 33⅔ scoreless innings streak ended. After splitting Games 2 and 3, the Giants won the next game 7-3 on Chuck Hiller's grand slam—the first by a National Leaguer in World Series play. Don Larsen—yes, *that* Don Larsen—earned the win in relief for San Francisco. New York regained the series lead

with a 5-3 victory in Game 5 made possible by Tom Tresh's three-run homer.

When the seesaw series moved back to San Francisco, a drenching rain caused three straight days of cancellations. When the skies cleared for Game 6, a rested Ford lost to Billy Pierce 5-2, setting up a deciding seventh game.

Right-hander Ralph Terry was the Yankees' starting pitcher in the tense finale. New York was clinging to a 1-0 lead in the bottom of the ninth inning, but the Giants had the tying and winning runs in scoring position. As Terry stood nervously on the mound at this anxious moment, he undoubtedly remembered that he had been in a similar situation before. Two Octobers earlier, Pittsburgh's Bill Mazeroski had led off the bottom of the ninth inning of Game 7 and hit a dramatic series-winning home run off him. Now Terry was facing another confrontation that would end with him as either a goat or a hero.

Ralph Terry (*center*), shown here accepting congratulations after his Game 5 victory, fared even better six days later when his Game 7 gem beat the Giants for the championship.

The imposing figure coming up to bat was the left-handed slugging Willie McCovey. Yankees manager Ralph Houk went to the mound to ask his pitcher if he preferred to intentionally walk McCovey and go after the next batter, right-handed hitting Orlando Cepeda. "I'd just as soon get it over now," Terry replied.

If Terry could get McCovey out, it would be his fall classic redemption. With two outs and the World Series on the line, Terry let fly a fastball. McCovey nailed it, smashing a blistering line drive that was heading like a bullet toward right field. But Yankees second baseman Bobby Richardson speared the ball for the final out.

"I really didn't have time to think about it," Richardson recalled. "It was just hit too hard."

The Yankees were champions for the second straight season and had captured the World Series flag for the 20th time in their history. Terry, who was named the MVP of the series, had

Above: Willie McCovey is swarmed by his Giants teammates as he returns to the dugout after blasting a solo home run that helped beat the Yankees 2-0 in Game 2. Big Mac could not have imagined the anguish that lay ahead in Game 7.

"He hit a good pitch good. The rest was in somebody else's hands. I was lucky."

—Yankees pitcher Ralph Terry, on Willie McCovey's screaming lineout that ended Game 7

atoned for his 1960 failure by shutting out the Giants on four hits in a nerve-wracking clinching game. Baseball, known as a game of inches, was surely that in the 1962 World Series.

McCovey's near-miss was immortalized by *Peanuts* cartoonist and anguished Giants fan Charles M. Schulz, in a strip in which a glum Charlie Brown laments: "Why couldn't McCovey have hit the ball just three feet higher?"

Top: AL Rookie of the Year Tom Tresh chases down a liner by Willie Mays in the seventh inning of Game 7. This terrific catch was especially painful to the Giants since Willie McCovey followed with a triple that would have tied the game.

Above: A lower reserved seat could be had for $8—a bargain for what turned into a closely contested 1962 World Series.

KOUFAX, DRYSDALE MOW DOWN BOMBERS

1963: Los Angeles 4, New York 0

The New York Yankees' 1963 World Series opponent was an old rival with a familiar nickname: the Dodgers. Except this time the Yankees were playing the *Los Angeles* Dodgers instead of the bums from Brooklyn.

The series was promoted as a matchup of the hard-hitting Yankees against the stingy Dodgers pitching, led by left-handed ace Sandy Koufax, a 25-game winner during the season. When a reporter asked Casey Stengel to predict a series winner, the former Yankees manager was noncommittal. "Good pitching will stop good hitting every time, or vice versa," he said. This time, pitching was king, as the Dodgers took four in a row by scores of 5-2, 4-1, 1-0, and 2-1.

The series opener at Yankee Stadium was a homecoming for the Brooklyn-born Koufax—and also his coming-out party. Koufax set a World Series record by striking out 15 batters. Johnny Podres, the 1955 series hero for Brooklyn,

won Game 2 with relief help from Ron Perranoski. The third game was the first World Series contest played at Dodger Stadium. There the Yankees and tough-luck loser Jim Bouton ran into a buzz saw named Don Drysdale, who hurled a 1-0 shutout.

The intimidating Drysdale, known for his brush-back pitches, allowed only three hits and one walk while striking out nine. "One of the greatest pitched games I ever saw," said Dodgers manager Walter Alston.

Ford and Koufax met again in Game 4. The premier lefties of their leagues had each given up a solo home run—Ford to Frank Howard, Koufax to Mickey Mantle—and were locked in a 1-1 tie in the seventh inning. In the bottom of the seventh, an error by Yankees rookie first baseman Joe Pepitone—he never saw Clete Boyer's thrown ball amid the white-shirted crowd—turned a sure out into what would prove to be the go-ahead run. With Koufax on the mound, a one-run lead was like money in the bank.

Thus, for the first time in history, the Yankees were swept in the World Series. Koufax was nearly unhittable in the series, pitching two complete games and allowing just three runs. He twice beat Yankees ace Whitey Ford—in the opener and the finale—and struck out a total of 23 batters while walking just three.

Yankees catcher Yogi Berra said of Koufax: "I can see how he won 25 games. What I don't understand is how he lost five."

Above: Series MVP Sandy Koufax was simply too much for the Yankees in the 1963 World Series. The sensational southpaw yielded just three earned runs while striking out 23 in two complete-game wins.

1963 World Series

Game 1

LAD	041 000 000	5 9 0
NYY	000 000 020	2 6 0

Game 2

LAD	200 100 010	4 10 1
NYY	000 000 001	1 7 0

Game 3

NYY	000 000 000	0 3 0
LAD	100 000 00x	1 4 1

Game 4

NYY	000 000 100	1 6 1
LAD	000 010 10x	2 2 1

CARDS CLOSE BOOK ON NY DYNASTY

1964: St. Louis 4, New York 3

Both the New York Yankees and St. Louis Cardinals made it to the 1964 World Series after heart-pounding pennant races. The Yankees, now skippered by Yogi Berra, rallied in September with an 11-game winning streak to clinch the American League pennant on the next-to-last day of the season. The Cardinals stole the National League title on the season's final day after Philadelphia blew a 6½ game lead with 12 games to go.

It was the second time in team history that the Yankees had made it to five straight World Series. Mickey Mantle, playing in his final fall classic, batted .333 with three home runs and eight RBI, and Bobby Richardson collected a record 13 hits in the series. But the Cardinals were not impressed, prevailing in seven tense games behind the overpowering pitching of Bob Gibson, who won twice.

After the teams split the first two games in St. Louis, Game 3 proved to be Mantle's defining World Series moment. The score was tied 1-1 going into the bottom of the ninth inning. Mantle was due to lead off against knuckleballing relief pitcher Barney Schultz. As the Mick was watching Schultz warm up, he turned to Elston Howard, the on-deck batter, and said, "You might as well go on in. I'm going to hit the first pitch I see out of the park."

Sure enough, Mantle deposited Schultz's first offering into the third deck of the right-field grandstand to win Game 3 and break a tie with Babe Ruth for career World Series homers. Mantle went deep twice more in the games that followed to set a mark of 18 series homers, which has yet to be equaled.

The longball was a big weapon for St. Louis, too. Ken Boyer's grand slam accounted for all the runs the Cards needed in a 4-3 victory in Game 4, and Tim McCarver's 10th-inning home run to win Game 5 gave them a three-games-to-two series edge heading back to St. Louis. The

It was power versus power when Bob Gibson pitched to Mickey Mantle in the 1964 World Series. Threes were wild: Mantle hit .333 with three homers in the series, while Gibson posted an ERA of 3.00 and fanned 31 in three starts.

1964 World Series

Game 1

NYY	030 010 010	5 12 2
STL	110 004 03x	9 12 0

Game 2

NYY	000 101 204	8 12 0
STL	001 000 011	3 7 0

Game 3

STL	000 010 000	1 6 0
NYY	010 000 001	2 5 2

Game 4

STL	000 004 000	4 6 1
NYY	300 000 000	3 6 1

Game 5

STL	000 020 000 3	5 10 1
NYY	000 000 002 0	2 6 2

Game 6

NYY	000 012 050	8 10 0
STL	100 000 011	3 10 1

Game 7

NYY	000 003 002	5 9 2
STL	000 330 10x	7 10 1

home runs continued to fly in Game 6 for the Yanks, as Joe Pepitone's grand slam forced a deciding seventh game.

The Bombers produced three home runs off Gibson in Game 7, but it was not enough to win the series. Pitching on two days' rest, Gibson outlasted rookie Mel Stottlemyre and hung on for a 7-5 win to give the Cardinals their first championship since 1946. St. Louis General Manager Branch Rickey was ecstatic. "It's the most champagne I've had in four years," he said in the celebratory locker room. "I'd rather beat the Yankees than any other team in baseball."

The loss turned out to be an omen for the great Yankees dynasty, which had begun in the 1920s with Ruth and Gehrig and peaked from 1947 to 1964. During those 18 postwar seasons, the Yankees won 15 AL pennants and 10 World Series. But after never having to wait more than four years to reach a World Series, the Bronx Bombers would not make it back again for 12 years. It was the end of an era.

Above left: Joe Pepitone crosses home plate after his eighth-inning grand slam in Game 6 helped set up a deciding seventh game at Busch Stadium. The young first baseman had driven in 100 runs in 1964 but would subsequently fall short of expectations.

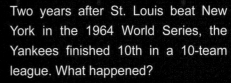

Two years after St. Louis beat New York in the 1964 World Series, the Yankees finished 10th in a 10-team league. What happened?

First, the Yankees replaced manager Yogi Berra with Johnny Keane, the Cardinals manager who had just beaten them in the '64 series days earlier. Keane wasn't respected by the veteran Yankees, who also had trouble staying healthy. Injuries beset Roger Maris, Mickey Mantle, Tony Kubek, and Elston Howard, and the Yanks fell to sixth place in 1965, their first sub-.500 finish in 40 years.

The amateur player draft, which began in 1965, had been designed to keep the wealthy Yankees from signing all the best available talent. It worked. Three-time 20-game winner Mel Stottlemyre, catcher Thurman Munson, and outfielder Bobby Murcer were among the team's few stars of the 1965–75 era.

Only in 1970 (93 wins) and 1974 (89) did New York exceed 83 wins. Following Ralph Houk's seven-year stint as skipper, Bill Virdon managed the Yankees in 1974 and 1975 before Billy Martin replaced him in August 1975. The volatile Martin then did what he did best—pushed a club to its full potential. The Bombers, who now were taking advantage of free agency, returned to the World Series in 1976, the year the renovated Yankee Stadium reopened.

Right: Many fans sensed that the 1964 series might be the last hurrah for the aging Yankees. Indeed, they would not return to the fall classic until 1976.

Below: Cardinals manager Johnny Keane gets clubhouse congratulations from his friend, Yogi Berra, after Game 7. Ironically, the Yankees would replace Berra with Keane a few days later.

CINCY SWINGS A BIG, RED BROOM

1976: Cincinnati 4, New York 0

The remodeled Yankee Stadium was unveiled in 1976, and just as they had in 1923, the New York Yankees christened their new stadium in grand style by winning a pennant. Chris Chambliss's dramatic home run in the last of the ninth inning against the Kansas City Royals in the decisive fifth game of the American League Championship Series sent the Yanks to the World Series for the first time since 1964.

The 1976 Yankees acted like the Yankees of old, winning 97 games to run away with the AL East division title by 10 ½. The Yankees were four seasons into the ownership reign of George Steinbrenner and in their first full season with former Yankees second baseman and World Series hero Billy Martin as manager. "The Yankees belonged in the World Series," Martin said before that year's fall classic. "That's the way it was when I played with the Yankees, and that's the way I want it to be as I manage the Yankees."

While the Yankees were playing in their 30th World Series, their opponent, Cincinnati, was baseball's Big Red Machine. Manager Sparky Anderson's club was the defending World Series champion and, after having won 102 games during the regular season, was drawing comparisons to the 1927 Yankees as a measuring stick for offensive firepower. With seven regulars batting over .300 for the series, the vaunted Reds had little trouble dispatching the Yankees in four games.

Cincinnati second baseman Joe Morgan homered in the bottom of the first inning of Game 1, and the Reds never looked back, steamrolling to 5-1, 4-3, 6-2, and 7-2 victories. Game 2 at Cincinnati's Riverfront Stadium was psychologically deflating for the Yanks. New York had its ace pitcher, high-priced free agent signee Jim "Catfish" Hunter, on the mound with the score tied 3-3 going into the bottom of the ninth inning. With two outs and nobody on, Ken Griffey Sr. bounced a groundball to Yankees shortstop

Thurman Munson prepares to slide safely under Johnny Bench's tag for a Game 4 run, but it was one of the few highlights for the Yankees against the Big Red Machine.

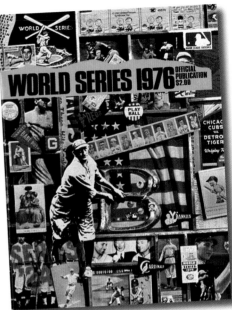

Fred Stanley, who threw wildly for a two-base error. Then Cincinnati first baseman Tony Perez lined Hunter's first pitch into left field for the game-winning hit.

Cincinnatti designated hitter Dan Driessen (this was the first World Series in which the DH was allowed) went 3-for-3 with a home run and a double in Game 3 at Yankee Stadium. Following the 6-2 defeat, Martin vowed that New York would win the next four in a row. The Yanks took a 1-0 lead in the first inning of the fourth game, but it would be their first and last lead in the series, as Cincinnati more than erased that deficit with a 7-2 final to complete the sweep.

"This won't happen again," said Martin. "We'll be a better team next year."

Reds catcher Johnny Bench was the star of the series, batting .533 with two home runs and six runs batted in. The one real bright spot for New York was its star catcher, Thurman Munson, who batted .529 with a series-best nine hits. Jim Mason, pinch-hitting for the Yanks in the seventh inning of Game 3, became the first player to homer in his only World Series at-bat.

1976 World Series

Game 1

NYY	010 000 000	1 5 1
CIN	101 001 20x	5 10 1

Game 2

NYY	000 100 200	3 9 1
CIN	030 000 001	4 10 0

Game 3

CIN	030 100 020	6 13 2
NYY	000 100 100	2 8 0

Game 4

CIN	000 300 004	7 9 2
NYY	100 010 000	2 8 0

"I never downgraded Johnny Bench. I'm a good ballplayer too, and I'd hit a ton in [his] ballpark. I'd do a lotta things Bench don't do. I'm not gonna give him anything and say I'm second best."

—Yankees catcher Thurman Munson, commenting on post-World Series buzz that Bench was the better backstop

Below: Johnny Bench clouts one of his two Game 4 home runs during a World Series in which he went 8-for-15 with six RBI. During the 1976 postseason, he ripped .444.

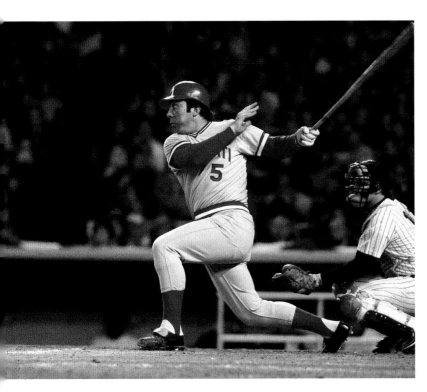

Even though the Reds swept the Yankees in the 1976 World Series, both teams' catchers—two of the best in the game—put on impressive offensive displays in the four games.

Cincinnati's Johnny Bench, a two-time NL MVP and MVP of the 1976 series, belted two homers and drove home six runs to lead all hitters. He batted .533 and slugged a ridiculous 1.133. His homer in Game 4's ninth inning sealed the deal for Cincy.

The Yankees' Thurman Munson didn't have Bench's power, but he was a productive hitter as well. The hardnosed team captain batted .302 with 17 homers and 105 RBI during the 1976 regular season to earn the AL MVP Award. In the World Series, he cracked nine hits to top all hitters and posted a snappy .529 average. Yet Reds manager Sparky Anderson issued a backhanded shot at Munson when, upon being asked about the two backstops, he replied, "I don't want to embarrass any catcher by comparing them to Johnny Bench."

Munson's life and career were tragically cut short when he crashed his personal jet on August 2, 1979. He died at age 32.

REG-GIE! REG-GIE! REG-GIE!

1977: New York 4, Los Angeles 2

When superstar free agent Reggie Jackson arrived in New York in 1977, the excitement level in the Bronx shot through the roof. The Yankees led the league in attendance (2,103,092), with many paying to see the new slugger with a swagger.

New York, which had won 100 games during the regular season, outlasted the Kansas City Royals in a taut playoff series. The Yankees scored three runs in the ninth inning of the fifth and final game to win 5-3. Though Jackson struggled against Kansas City in the League Championship Series, he made the World Series his personal stage, batting .450 with five home runs and eight runs batted in. The Yankees defeated the Los Angeles Dodgers in six games, and Jackson's performance in the finale—when he blasted three home runs—was one of the most memorable in postseason history.

The Yankees, anxious to atone for their disappointing performance against the Reds in the 1976 fall classic, got off to a promising start when the series opened in New York. They pulled off a 4-3 win in 12 innings on a double by Willie Randolph and a single by Paul Blair. Rookie manager Tom Lasorda's Dodgers featured a hard-hitting lineup that included Steve Garvey, Ron Cey, Reggie Smith, and Dusty Baker—the first foursome to each hit at least 30 homers in a season. In Game 2, the Dodgers lived up to their reputation, tagging four home runs as starting pitcher Burt Hooton coasted to a 6-1 win.

The series moved to Los Angeles, where the Yankees prevailed 5-3 behind pitcher Mike Torrez. The next day, Ron Guidry went the distance in a 4-2 win—backed by a Jackson home run—for a three-games-to-one Yankees lead. The Dodgers sent the series back to New York with a 10-4 win behind Don Sutton, although Jackson again went deep.

Game 6 was the Reggie Jackson show, and what he accomplished at Yankee Stadium that night may never be

Reggie Jackson eyes the flight of his third home run of Game 6. It was Jackson's fourth homer in as many at-bats (not including a walk) and his fifth of the 1977 World Series.

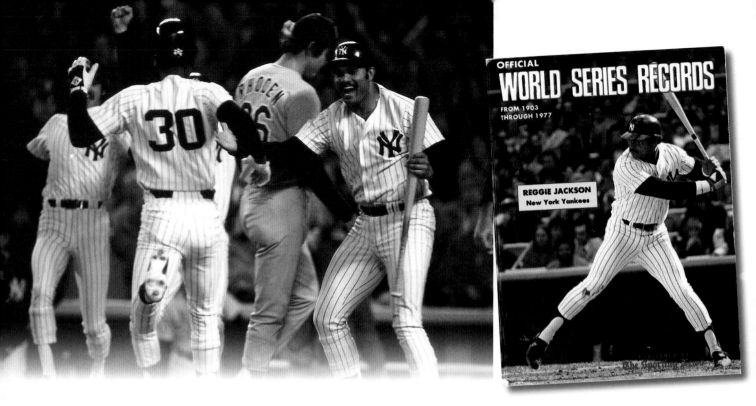

OFFICIAL WORLD SERIES RECORDS

FROM 1903 THROUGH 1977

REGGIE JACKSON
New York Yankees

approached. The beauty of Jackson's performance was that he blasted each of his three home runs on the first pitch against three different pitchers. He victimized Hooton in the fourth inning and hit a rocket off Elias Sosa in the fifth that left the park in the blink of an eye. "I overwhelmed that baseball by the sheer force of my will," he said.

His third home run, in the eighth inning, was a solo shot off a Charlie Hough knuckleball that landed deep into the far-away bleachers in right-center field. "I must admit," said Dodgers first baseman Steve Garvey, "when Reggie hit his third home run and I was sure nobody was looking, I applauded in my glove."

As Jackson crossed home plate, the 56,407 exuberant hometown fans paid tribute to one of the greatest individual performances in baseball history by screaming "Reg-gie! Reg-gie! Reg-gie!" until their hero popped out of the dugout for a curtain call, nodding to the appreciative crowd. He became the only player besides Babe Ruth to hit three home runs in a World Series game. His five homers for the series also set a fall classic record.

Jackson's performance in the clinching game made it easy for Mike Torrez to go the distance in an 8-4 victory. The triumph marked New York's first World Series title since 1962.

Above left: Willie Randolph scores the winning run in the 12th inning of the opener. Randolph doubled and scored on a single by Paul Blair to give New York a 4-3 win.

Above right: Yankees slugger Reggie Jackson became the cover boy for this World Series record book after his performance in the 1977 fall classic.

Opposite page: Game 7 winner Mike Torrez, who twice beat the Dodgers with complete games, and catcher Thurman Munson celebrate the Yankees' first world championship since 1962.

"Save some of those for the game."

"No problem. There are more where those came from."

—Game 6 batting practice conversation between Willie Randolph and Reggie Jackson after Randolph watched the slugger belt numerous balls into the seats

1977 World Series

Game 1

LA	200 000 001 000	3 6 0
NYY	100 001 010 001	4 11 0

Game 2

LA	212 000 001	6 9 0
NYY	000 100 000	1 5 0

Game 3

NYY	300 110 000	5 10 0
LA	003 000 000	3 7 1

Game 4

NYY	030 001 000	4 7 0
LA	002 000 000	2 4 0

Game 5

NYY	000 000 220	4 9 2
LA	100 432 00x	10 13 0

Game 6

LA	201 000 001	4 9 0
NYY	020 320 01x	8 8 1

Reggie Jackson

When the Yankees signed free agent Reggie Jackson to a then-record $2.96 million, five-year contract after the 1976 season, they figured they had landed a jewel. The 30-year-old outfielder's résumé already featured one AL MVP title (plus three other appearances in the top five in voting), two homer crowns, one RBI championship, and three slugging average titles to go along with six All-Star selections. But perhaps the Yankees' management also noted Mr. Jackson's performance in the postseason.

At that point in his career, Reggie had played in 32 postseason games—all with Oakland, with whom he had won three world titles. Four times his OPS had surpassed .940 in a postseason series. There was no doubt that Reggie loved the big stage. He said that if he played in New York, they would name a candy bar for him. In 1978, Standard Brands took him up on it.

The well-known nickname came about in the 1977 ALCS when Jackson, benched by manager Billy Martin, came back to deliver a clutch pinch-hit single in the eighth inning. "Mr. October," Billy sneered. Ignoring the sarcasm, Reggie lovingly claimed the nickname for his own.

Jackson also added his brains (and hip) to a critical play in the 1978 World Series. The Dodgers were leading the fourth game 3-1 (and the series 2-1) in the sixth inning when, with Reggie on first, Lou Piniella popped a slow liner that Dodger shortstop Bill Russell dropped in an attempt to create an inning-ending double play. As Russell threw to first, Reggie stuck out his hip. The ball caromed into the outfield, and the Yanks rallied to a series-tying victory.

For his career, Reggie Jackson was a World Series smash, with a .357 average, 10 homers, and 24 RBI in 27 games.

George Steinbrenner with coach Yogi Berra and manager Billy Martin, after clinching the 1976 AL pennant

The 1977 Yankees earned their humorous nickname, the "Bronx Zoo," because they acted like a bunch of wild animals when caged in the clubhouse. Other teams had spats or bickering cliques, but with these Yanks it was all-out warfare. This cluster of erratic, irascible, scowling, sulking, pampered athletes just didn't get along.

Presiding over this motley crew were two men: the bossy, meddling, imperious owner George Steinbrenner and the field manager, bullying tough guy Billy Martin. At the center of the cauldron was outfielder Reggie Jackson, signed to a multimillion-dollar contract, whose bravado matched his substantial batting talent. As one writer put it, "Every Yankee, it seemed, hated Martin and Jackson. And Martin and Jackson hated each other." The shinola hit the air conditioner on June 18, 1977, when, during a nationally televised Saturday afternoon game, Martin yanked Jackson from the field in the middle of an inning, and the two nearly came to blows in the dugout.

All was forgiven that fall. After Jackson's three home runs in Game 6 of the World Series, he and Martin were arm-in-arm in the clubhouse. Winning 100 games in 1978 thanks to a 25-3 season from Ron "Louisiana Lightning" Guidry, New York then took out Kansas City in the playoffs for the third straight year. Come October, the nation delighted in watching this "soap opera" in prime time.

Things changed in July of the next year when Martin said of Reggie and George, "One's a born liar, the other's convicted," which cost him his job, at least for the time being. (Steinbrenner would hire him back four more times.) The nickname "Bronx Zoo" wasn't applied to them until 1979, with the publication of Yankees reliever Sparky Lyle's memoir of the same name, which covered the 1977 and '78 seasons. The book's editor is given credit for the coinage.

REGGIE, BUCKY DO IN DODGERS

1978: New York 4, Los Angeles 2

The tumultuous atmosphere in the Yankees' clubhouse didn't change in 1978, and neither did the end result: a World Series championship for New York in six games over the Los Angeles Dodgers. But this time, the Bombers overcame a two-games-to-none deficit by winning four straight games for the title. No team in World Series history had ever done that.

These Yankees were no strangers to comebacks. Trailing the division-leading Red Sox by 14 games in late July, the Yankees stormed back under manager Bob Lemon to end the season in a tie with Boston. After defeating the Red Sox in a dramatic one-game playoff (thanks to Bucky Dent's home run over Fenway Park's Green Monster), New York then ousted the Kansas City Royals in the League Championship Series to advance to the World Series for the third consecutive year. They faced a Dodgers team that had led the majors in ERA and the National League in homers.

The Dodgers won the first two World Series games in Los Angeles, 11-5 and 4-3. The second game featured a nerve-wracking confrontation between rookie pitcher Bob Welch and star outfielder Reggie Jackson, who had murdered the Dodgers in the previous year's World Series. In the ninth inning, with two runners on base and two outs, Jackson battled Welch for nine pitches before fanning to end the game. "It was a great at-bat," Jackson said. "I enjoyed every pitch except the last."

The New Yorkers came home to the Bronx and sent left-hander Ron Guidry to the mound in a must-win game. Guidry, coming off an otherworldly 25-3 season, wasn't sharp, allowing eight hits and seven walks. Yet he went the distance in a 5-1 victory, bailed out by the glove work of Graig Nettles, who made four dazzling stops at third base to squelch the Dodgers' hopes. "Every time I put my glove down, a ball seemed to jump into it," Nettles said.

Goose Gossage (54) pulls World Series MVP Bucky Dent along to the Yankees clubhouse after Dent completed his surprising 10-for-24, seven-RBI performance against the Dodgers.

Left: Dodgers catcher Steve Yeager celebrates after Reggie Jackson's tense, nine-pitch duel with Bob Welch ended in a ninth-inning strikeout that concluded Game 2. Jackson left the tying and winning runs on base.

The Yankees needed 10 innings to win Game 4, secured by Lou Piniella's game-winning hit. Jackson, ever in the middle of it all for the Yankees, made an impact in this game with his guile in the sixth inning, breaking up a double play by getting in the way of Bill Russell's throw to first. The ball hit Jackson in the hip and caromed into right field, allowing a pivotal run to score. Los Angeles manager Tom Lasorda protested that Jackson intentionally interfered with the ball, but umpires weren't buying it. "I didn't do anything but stand there," Jackson said.

New York blasted Los Angeles 12-2 with an 18-hit barrage in Game 5, as rookie Jim Beattie pitched a complete game and Thurman Munson led the way with five runs batted in. In the decisive sixth game at Dodger Stadium, Catfish Hunter pitched seven innings and Goose Gossage shut the door on the Dodgers for a relatively easy 7-2 Yankees win and a second consecutive World Series championship.

The big blow of the game was Jackson's 430-foot home run off Welch. Reggie hit .391 with two homers and eight RBI in the series, but the Yankees won the trophy thanks in large part to the hitting of two men at the bottom of the order. Brian Doyle, substituting at second base for the injured Willie Randolph, batted .438, and shortstop Dent, the World Series MVP, batted .417 with seven runs batted in.

1978 World Series

Game 1

NYY	000 000 320	5	9	1
LA	030 310 31x	11	15	2

Game 2

NYY	002 000 100	3	11	0
LA	000 103 00x	4	7	0

Game 3

LA	001 000 000	1	8	0
NYY	110 000 30x	5	10	1

Game 4

LA	000 030 000 0	3	6	1
NYY	000 002 010 1	4	9	0

Game 5

LA	101 000 000	2	9	3
NYY	004 300 41x	12	18	0

Game 6

NYY	030 002 200	7	11	0
LA	101 000 000	2	7	1

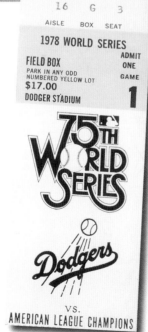

Above left: Graig Nettles, who set a new standard for third base defense in the World Series, makes a ridiculous catch to rob L.A. of a hit in Game 5.

Above right: Catcher Thurman Munson congratulates Ron Guidry on his complete-game Game 3 victory at Yankee Stadium. Guidry, who went 25-3 during the season, gave up just a third-inning run in the win.

Right: It was somehow fitting that the 75th anniversary of the World Series featured the showcase's top rivalry: Yankees versus Dodgers.

16   G   3
AISLE   BOX   SEAT

1978 WORLD SERIES

FIELD BOX   ADMIT
PARK IN ANY ODD   ONE
NUMBERED YELLOW LOT   GAME
$17.00
DODGER STADIUM   1

75TH
WORLD
SERIES

Dodgers

VS.
AMERICAN LEAGUE CHAMPIONS

"Nobody's ever done what this club did. This is as great a Yankee team as there ever was. I don't care about the '27 Yankees or any other of the great Yankee teams. This team overcame everything."

—Yankees owner George Steinbrenner, referring to how his team overcame internal squabbles and a two-game deficit in the World Series

Boss Blows Top After Series Fiasco

1981: Los Angeles 4, New York 2

The Yankees made headlines during the 1981 World Series for all the wrong reasons. It appeared that the Bombers would breeze to a series triumph against the Los Angeles Dodgers when they won the first two games at Yankee Stadium by scores of 5-3 and 3-0. But then the roof caved in on manager Bob Lemon's boys, and they blew the next four games by scores of 5-4, 8-7, and 2-1 at Dodger Stadium and a lopsided 9-2 score in Game 6 at Yankee Stadium.

Luckless Yankees relief pitcher George Frazier was charged with the loss in three of those games, setting an ignominious record for most losses in a six-game series. High-priced free agent Dave Winfield had troubles of his own in the series. He managed just one single in 22 at-bats for an almost invisible .045 average and was labeled "Mr. May" by owner George Steinbrenner for his ill-timed slump. In an embarrassing incident, an angry Steinbrenner

was allegedly involved in a fracas with Dodgers fans in a Los Angeles hotel elevator after his team lost the fifth game.

The series had gotten off to a promising start for the Yankees. Bob Watson hit a first-inning three-run homer to stake starter Ron Guidry an early lead in the opener. In Game 2, crafty lefty Tommy John, who had pitched for the Dodgers against New York in the 1977 and 1978 World Series, stymied his old teammates for seven innings. Rich "Goose" Gossage completed the shutout for his second save in two days. "Every series win is satisfying," said John, "but there was something very special getting back at the Dodgers after they decided I couldn't help them anymore."

The Yankees had an aura of invincibility as the series moved to Los Angeles, and the Dodgers were reeling. Manager Tom Lasorda turned to rookie sensation Fernando Valenzuela in Game 3, and although he allowed nine hits and seven walks,

When Yankees owner George Steinbrenner signed Dave Winfield to an unprecedented 10-year, $23 million contract prior to the 1981 season, he expected much more than the .045 batting average (1-for-22) the All-Star outfielder produced in that year's World Series.

Valenzuela came away with the victory. "He didn't have good stuff, but it was one of the gutsiest performances I've ever seen," Lasorda said.

The next day, the Dodgers evened the series with another close win, and in Game 5, for the third day in a row, L.A. overcame a Yankees lead to grab a one-run victory. The Dodgers were one win away from the title, but Lemon was not conceding. "All we need is a two-game winning streak at home," the Yankees skipper said. "We've done that before."

The final game was tied 1-1 in the fourth inning when Lemon decided to pinch-hit for John, his dependable starter, with two on and two out. The controversial decision backfired when Bobby Murcer flied out. Frazier and the bullpen subsequently imploded as the Dodgers made it four wins in a row to take the series.

Afterward, an irritated Steinbrenner issued a public apology to all Yankees fans. Despite the mea culpa, the 1981 World Series loss marked the beginning of a frustrating era in which they would not win a pennant for 15 years, the Yankees' longest drought since they first reached the fall classic in 1921.

Above: Wily left-hander Tommy John was outstanding for New York in the 1981 World Series, yielding just one earned run in 13 innings of work over three games. Yankees reliever George Frazier (0-3, 17.18 ERA) was the goat of the series.

"I want to sincerely apologize to the people of New York and to fans of the New York Yankees everywhere for the performance of the Yankee team in the World Series."

—Yankees owner George Steinbrenner

Above: Not even a major league players' strike in 1981 could keep the Yankees from adding another pennant to their collection.

Below: Bill Russell of the Dodgers tags out Aurelio Rodriguez (the original A-Rod!) at second base in the seventh inning of Game 4, one of three straight one-run wins for Los Angeles.

When play resumed on August 10, 1981, after a two-month-long players strike, four teams, including the Yankees, were guaranteed playoff berths. That's because the owners decided on a split-season playoff format, with the four division leaders of the first half (pre-strike) and the four division winners of the second half (post-strike) making the playoffs.

Yankees manager Gene Michael was not happy. For the rest of the season, his team had absolutely nothing to play for. "It should be a bye" for winning both halves, Michael insisted. Yankees pitcher Rudy May was blunt: "I still don't think it's fair that we're automatically in there."

The Yankees performed like it didn't matter, finishing sixth in the second half. Michael was replaced in September by Bob Lemon, who wound up beating Milwaukee in the first round of the playoffs and then sweeping Oakland in the ALCS. In the National League, however, the Reds had the best overall record in baseball yet failed to reach the postseason because different teams had edged them out in each half. The Cardinals had the best overall record in the NL East and were left out of the playoffs.

It was a year that made little sense any way you looked at it.

YOUNG YANKEES
SHOW NO QUIT

1996: New York 4, Atlanta 2

The 1996 Yankees put the "New" in New York. The players' lack of World Series experience did not bother them in the least against the defending champion Atlanta Braves and the most imposing pitching staff in baseball. On the contrary, the Yankees seemed to thrive in pressure situations against a team that appeared destined to repeat—and the result was the end of the franchise's longest World Series title drought since their first crown in 1923.

It had been 18 years since the Yankees had won a World Series. Their longest previous dry spell since '23 had been from 1962 to '77. And it looked for a while like the 1996 title would not only go to the Braves, but would do so quickly and convincingly.

Atlanta was powered by the best pitching in the game. John Smoltz, Tom Glavine, and Greg Maddux—all potential Hall of Famers—topped a rotation that dominated the National League. If the Braves could put a few runs on the board, they were virtually certain of victory. At least that's the way their season had been playing out, and it was certainly the way the 1996 World Series began.

Smoltz was an easy winner over Andy Pettitte in the opener, 12-1, at Yankee Stadium in a game delayed one day by a storm. Adding insult to embarrassment for the Yankees, the Braves' 19-year-old Andruw Jones broke Mickey Mantle's record by becoming the youngest player ever to hit a World Series home run. In fact, he hit two in the game.

Maddux was masterful in Game 2. The four-time Cy Young Award winner blanked the Yankees on six hits over eight innings, and Mark Wohlers retired the hosts in the ninth. In World Series history, only two teams had ever come back to win after dropping the first two games at home—and neither of those clubs had to face three straight

Catcher Joe Girardi's triple in the third inning of Game 6 drove in a run, and he later scored from third. The Yankees' three-run rally that inning was all they needed in a 3-2, title-clinching victory over the Braves.

road games against the dominant pitching the Braves possessed.

"I don't know any words of wisdom when you go down 0-2 against the defending world champions," said David Cone, New York's Game 3 starter.

The Yankees did not need wisdom as badly as they needed some hits, and they got big ones from one of their youngsters in Cone's 5-2 win. Bernie Williams, who along with fellow 20-somethings Derek Jeter and Tino Martinez had been sparking the Yankees all year, singled home an early run off Glavine and added a two-run homer in the eighth inning.

The following night, it was high-scoring drama that pulled New York even. Atlanta squandered a 6-0 lead late, and Jim Leyritz hit a game-tying home run off Wohlers in the eighth. A bases-loaded walk to Wade Boggs and a Braves error in the 10th made the difference in the Yankees' 8-6 win, and all of a sudden Atlanta was reeling.

"We've been doing this all season," said Boggs, who called it the biggest walk of his 15-year career to that point. "It's not like we just started inventing comebacks in the playoffs."

Pettitte earned redemption in a 1-0 Game 5 shutout that sent New York

Above: Braves outfielder Andruw Jones, just 19 years old, supplanted Mickey Mantle as the youngest player ever to hit a World Series home run. Jones went deep not once but twice in Game 1.

Opposite page: Jim Leyritz strokes a three-run, game-tying homer in the eighth inning of Game 4, a contest that saw the Yankees overcome a six-run deficit to tie the series at two games apiece.

back home with an improbable 3-2 series lead. He yielded just five hits while pitching into the ninth inning, with his only run support coming on Cecil Fielder's RBI double off Smoltz in the fourth.

The turnaround was an emotional one for Yankees manager Joe Torre. Throughout the playoffs, the health of his brother Frank had grown worse as he awaited a heart transplant at a New York hospital. Joe visited him often, ran baseball decisions past the former major leaguer, and asked fans for prayers. No one was happier than the Torre family that the Yankees were returning home in better spirits than when they had left a few days earlier, and their joy reached a pinnacle on October 26.

In the only home-team victory of the series, New York got all three of its runs off Maddux on four hits in the third inning. The big blow was Joe Girardi's RBI triple. The Braves got to Jimmy Key for a run in the fourth and added another in the ninth to set up a dramatic finish. But closer John Wetteland chalked up his fourth save in as many games to wrap up the game, the world title, and MVP honors.

"They [the Braves] said they could beat the '27 Yankees. But they forgot about the '96 Yankees."

—Yankees catcher Joe Girardi, after defeating Atlanta in the World Series

WORLD SERIES CHAMPIONS
NEW YORK YANKEES
1996

Above: It had been 18 long years since the Yankees had hoisted a World Series championship trophy—their longest drought since winning their first in 1923.

Left: The long wait for a championship ended in 1996 for Wade Boggs, who took a celebratory ride on a police horse after adding a World Series crown to his résumé. During the regular season, Boggs had hit over .300 for the 14th time in his Hall of Fame career.

Derek Jeter and Joe Torre

They will forever be known as the "Torre-Jeter years," the dozen seasons of excellence from 1996 through 2007 in which the Yanks finished first in the AL East 10 times, placed second twice, appeared in six World Series, and brought home four world titles.

In 1996, Joe Torre might have seemed an unlikely choice as Yankees manager. The press called him "Clueless Joe." In 14 previous years of managerial duty, his teams had just a .470 winning percentage, with one first-place and two second-place finishes.

Torre was inheriting a Yankees team that had only one postseason appearance in the previous 14 years and had finished a most un-Yankee-like fifth or worse five times. It could be said that Torre's success with the Yanks was attributable less to his handling of talent than to his manipulation of the oft-ravenous New York media, preventing them from turning offhand clubhouse comments into divisive front-page news.

Rookie Derek Jeter became the starting short-stop in the first game of the Torre regime. It was immediately obvious that he was something special. From 1996 to 2000, when the Bombers won four world titles, Jeter—whose boyhood dream was to play shortstop for the Yankees—led the league in hits and runs once and posted a .323 average over the five seasons. During that period, he also batted over .400 in four different postseason series. But more than just a superb ballplayer, Jeter had an element of class, of pride, of confidence and determination that seems to be the attribute that sets Yankees greats apart from all others.

Of course, Jeter wasn't the only Yankees All-Star of the late 1990s. Andy Pettitte, Bernie Williams, Jorge Posada, Tino Martinez, and Paul O'Neill were among the best at their positions, and Mariano Rivera established himself as perhaps the greatest relief pitcher of all time. But at the heart of this dynasty were the contributions of No. 2 and No. 6, Torre and Jeter. Interestingly, those are the only single-digit Yankees uniform numbers that are not retired—at least not yet.

SWEEP CAPS 125-WIN SEASON

1998: New York 4, San Diego 0

The outcome of the 1998 World Series was a foregone conclusion. The only debate would come during the aftermath, in the form of this question: Were the 1998 Yankees the greatest team ever?

Few seemed ready to make that leap, and the shadow of the Ruth-and-Gehrig-led 1927 Yankees might render the '98 juggernaut only the second-best team in *franchise* history. Still, New York's 114 regular-season wins (which broke Cleveland's AL record of 111) and 11-2 postseason record made the Yankees the winningest team ever and put them squarely in the conversation.

"I can't see anybody dominating the league the way we did," shortstop Derek Jeter said. "I mean, 125-50? That's ridiculous."

"I don't think they have a weakness," raved San Diego General Manager Kevin Towers after seeing his club outscored 26-13 in the World Series. "They have experience

and youth, they play good defense, they have speed, they take the extra base, they have power, they have good at-bats, they have terrific pitching, they have a manager who's had success, and they have money. I don't know what else there is."

Some, at the time, called these Yankees a team without superstars. In retrospect, they were a team whose superstars were just beginning to emerge.

Dominant closer Mariano Rivera saved all three "close" games of New York's World Series sweep of San Diego, securing wins in Game 1 (9-6), Game 3 (5-4), and Game 4 (3-0). Bernie Williams and Jorge Posada homered in the most one-sided contest, a 9-3 romp at Yankee Stadium in Game 2. Tino Martinez batted .385 and Chuck Knoblauch .375 for the series, while Jeter turned in a .353 average.

Even the Yankees' role players came through, none more impressively than Scott Brosius. A little-known utility man for seven years with Oakland, Brosius joined the Bronx

World Series MVP Scott Brosius celebrates his winning home run off Trevor Hoffman in Game 3. Brosius homered twice, collected eight hits, and drove in six runs in the series.

1998 World Series

Game 1
| SD | 002 030 010 | 6 8 1 |
| NYY | 020 000 70x | 9 9 1 |

Game 2
| SD | 000 010°020 | 3 10 1 |
| NYY | 331 020 00x | 9 16 0 |

Game 3
| NYY | 000 000 230 | 5 9 1 |
| SD | 000 003 010 | 4 7 1 |

Game 4
| NYY | 000 001 020 | 3 9 0 |
| SD | 000 000 000 | 0 7 0 |

Above left: Tino Martinez hits a Game 1 grand slam to highlight a seven-run seventh inning for the Yankees, who knocked the Padres on their heels with a come-from-behind triumph.

Below: *Time* magazine held nothing back in its lauding of the 1998 Yankees, who followed a 114-win regular season with a dominant playoff run—11 wins in 13 games.

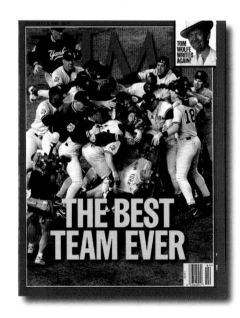

Bombers before the season and became an All-Star for the first time. He turned his first playoff experience into a showcase, hitting .400 against Texas in the ALDS and .300 against Cleveland in the ALCS. He was even better under World Series pressure.

Leading Game 3 by a 3-2 score on their home field and with major league saves leader Trevor Hoffman on the mound in the eighth inning, the Padres seemed poised to climb right back into the series. Brosius had other ideas. The third baseman stayed off Hoffman's devastating change-ups, waited for a fastball, and knocked it out of Qualcomm Stadium for a three-run homer that made 5-4 winners of the Yankees. Brosius was selected World Series MVP after hitting .471 with two homers.

Between their quick sweep of the NL champs and their tickertape parade, there was plenty of time for debate about whether this was the greatest team of all time. The 1998 Yankees had scored more runs than any team in the majors, allowed the fewest runs in the AL, and won well over 70 percent of their games. Former Yankees great Reggie Jackson weighed in, saying he would leave the final decision to the historians.

"But 125 games, man," he added. "That's a number. They put up a mark. It's really fantastic."

"[They] never bashed anybody's head or danced on anybody's grave. They went about their business, [and] they demonstrated respect for the other players."

—Yankees General Manager Brian Cashman, after the 1998 season

Below: Untouchable reliever Mariano Rivera, king of the cut fastball, celebrates his series-clinching save with catcher Joe Girardi. Rivera notched six postseason saves in 1998 while not allowing a run—a feat he would equal in 1999.

Mariano Rivera has piled up statistics that firmly ensconce him as one of the greatest relief pitchers of all time. He has accomplished this with the aid of two amazing tools: a wicked cut fastball and an almost Zen-like serenity on the mound (this when most closers seem ready to burst from their intensity).

With that cutter, called "the best single pitch ever" and "the most dominant pitch of a generation" by fellow major leaguers, Rivera uses its wicked late break to terrify left-handed hitters. Facing Rivera in the 1999 World Series, Atlanta's Ryan Klesko broke three bats in one plate appearance.

Like other Yankees greats, Rivera saves his best for last. Entering 2010, he was perched atop the postseason leader board with 39 saves—23 more than anyone else. He also was first in games (88) and ERA (0.74) and second in winning percentage (.889; 8-1). From 1997 to 2000, he threw 34 ⅓ consecutive shutout innings in the postseason, breaking Whitey Ford's major league record.

BROOM AND DOOM FOR BRAVES

1999: New York 4, Atlanta 0

In the final inning of the Yankees' third World Series championship in four years, the team's newest star watched in awe from the dugout as his clinching Game 4 victory was preserved by "automatic" closer Mariano Rivera. "This must be what it's like to be a Yankee," pitcher Roger Clemens said.

Donning the pinstripes put Clemens in position to win his first World Series game and put an elusive championship on his résumé. It further proved New York's commitment to staying on top. And it cemented the championship legacies of such regulars as Derek Jeter, Bernie Williams, Tino Martinez, Jorge Posada, and Andy Pettitte, among many others.

In the opposite dugout, the Atlanta Braves—perhaps in better position than even the Yankees to claim "Team of the '90s" status—felt the sting of conceding that title to the Bronx Bombers. It was the second time in four years that

the Braves had been defeated by the Yankees in a World Series, and it was their fourth World Series setback of the decade.

"They ought to be in a higher league somewhere," Atlanta pitcher John Smoltz said.

It was their lack of offense that doomed the Braves. They scored only once in two of the four games and managed just two runs in another, giving their talented starting rotation precious little support.

The Yankees, of course, had plenty to do with that. Orlando Hernandez allowed one hit in seven innings in the opener, a 4-1 decision at Turner Field. The following night, David Cone was backed by a 14-hit barrage while blanking the Braves over seven innings in a 7-2 win.

Yes, the Yankees were mighty, but they were also charmed. Every move made by manager Joe Torre, who had been treated for prostate cancer in the spring, seemed to be the right one come October.

Mariano Rivera was Mr. Automatic once again in 1999, earning a victory and two saves in three scoreless appearances as the Yankees dominated the Braves.

For example, Torre gave outfielder Chad Curtis his only World Series start in Game 3 against Tom Glavine, the Braves ace who had missed starting the opener because of flu symptoms. In front of a crazed home crowd, Curtis hit two home runs in the game, including the walk-off winner in the bottom of the 10th inning.

After that, it was only a matter of whether the Braves could muster even one win before bowing out. And the answer was a resounding no.

Clemens made certain of that, yielding just four hits over 7⅔ innings of the final victory. Rivera's save was his second of the set. He also earned the Game 3 victory in relief, did not allow a run in any of his three appearances, and was named World Series Most Valuable Player.

New York became the first team to record successive World Series sweeps since the 1938-39 Yankees did it.

"I've been to other stadiums, and they've got banners hanging around that say 'Wild Card Champions' and 'Division Champions' or whatever," veteran Chili Davis said, noting that New York judges success only in World Series titles. "But here, they don't even hang those banners up. I think they're in the batting cage or somewhere like that."

Above: Unlikely hero Chad Curtis is carried off the field after socking a game-winning, 10th-inning home run against the Braves in Game 3 at Yankee Stadium. Curtis was a part-time outfielder for the Yankees.

Left: Normally the last person to gloat, Mariano Rivera couldn't help touting a broom (as well as the flag of his native Panama) after the Yankees' second consecutive World Series sweep.

Below: Superstar hurler Roger Clemens didn't pitch until the fourth game of the 1999 World Series, but it was worth the wait. The Rocket allowed just one run in the clinching game to secure his first world championship.

An initial analysis of the Yankees' 14-game World Series winning streak, 1996 to 2000, might leave you scratching your head. In one of those series, New York was actually outscored by eight runs and outhit .254 to .216. Sure, the core of the Yanks' order routinely batted .300 or better in those series. Their pitching contained at least a couple of future Hall of Famers, and their infield defense in particular was nonpareil.

But these weren't the Bronx Bashers of old. They were more likely to win with a heads-up extra-base sprint than with a clutch longball (although a big homer was never out of the question). The wizened Yanks were patient and poised at the plate; for example, they drew 15 walks to the Mets' 1 in the first two games of the 2000 World Series. The plentitude of baserunners allowed them to string together three runs or more in an inning in 11 of the 14 games.

During the streak, the New Yorkers scored 11 unearned runs. It was more than being opportunistic. What made this Yankees team great was simple. If you made a mistake, they made you pay.

A Three-Peat
at the Mets' Expense

2000: NY Yankees 4, NY Mets 1

New York's subway system, to those unfamiliar with it, can seem a confused confluence of colored lines connecting one borough to the next. You can get from Point A to Point B, but a map, some guidance, and a little patience come in handy. The 2000 "Subway Series," on the other hand, was considerably easier to sort out.

Though each game was decided by a mere one or two runs, the Yankees continued their fast track to baseball history, putting away the Mets in five to capture their third consecutive World Series title and fourth in five years under manager Joe Torre.

Surmised Yankees owner George Steinbrenner: "This core group, winning four World Series out of five years in this day and age, when you have to come through layer after layer of postseason play, we can put our record, our dedication, our resolve against any team that has ever played the game of baseball."

It was the first time since the Yankees and Brooklyn Dodgers tangled in 1956 that the city of New York celebrated a Subway Series, and the buzz was palpable. The Mets had finished second to the Braves in the NL East, but the wild card qualifiers had won seven more games than the Yankees during the season.

The Yankees had won 12 consecutive World Series games, a number they stretched to an unprecedented 14 in a row with 4-3 and 6-5 victories at Yankee Stadium to start the 2000 series. The opener required 4 hours, 51 minutes to decide—the longest game in World Series history. Chuck Knoblauch tied it for the Yankees on a sacrifice fly in the bottom of the ninth, and surprise starter Jose Vizcaino ended it with an RBI single in the 12th to cap his four-hit night.

Game 2 featured an anticipated showdown between Mets superstar catcher Mike Piazza and Yankees starter Roger Clemens. The two had made little effort to hide their disdain for one another since Clemens had hit Piazza

Jose Vizcaino (*right*) leaps into the arms of Derek Jeter after his 12th-inning single won the opener and sent the Yankees racing toward their 26th World Series championship.

in the helmet with a pitch in July. This time, Piazza broke his bat on a Clemens pitch in the first inning, and a portion of the wood skipped toward the mound. Clemens picked it up and threw it toward the Mets dugout—not far from Piazza—and the benches emptied. Order was restored, and the Yankees jumped to a 6-0 lead before holding on for a 6-5 win.

Though the Mets won just one game in the series, they ended two long streaks in doing so. Their 4-2 victory in Game 3 not only stopped the Yanks' 14-game

World Series winning streak but gave Orlando Hernandez his first career postseason loss. "El Duque" had gone 8-0 in his nine previous postseason starts.

The Subway Series, though, never reached a second travel day. Derek Jeter homered in each of the final two games at Shea Stadium, sparking 3-2 and 4-2 wins. Jeter, just 26 years old, set a five-game World Series record with 19 total bases while winning the MVP Award and his fourth championship ring. He hit .409 with two homers and five extra-base hits.

Above: There was no love lost between the Mets' Mike Piazza and the Yankees' Roger Clemens before and after this memorable bat-throwing episode in Game 2. Back in July, Clemens had beaned Piazza with a blazing fastball.

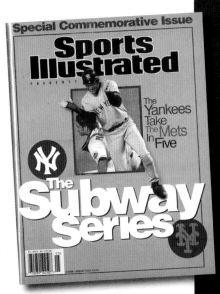

Right: *Sports Illustrated* commemorated the Subway Series with this special issue, which few Mets fans had the stomach to purchase.

Below: Jorge Posada takes one on the hip while sliding home in the ninth inning of Game 5. Posada's run gave the Yanks a 3-2 lead, and the bounding ball allowed Scott Brosius to score, too. Mariano Rivera slammed the door to secure the 4-2, title-clinching win.

Nobody in New York slept well during the 2000 Subway Series. The Mets and Yankees had been playing interleague games since 1997—all 18 games sold out, with 11 of them ending in Yankee wins. But as frenzied as those games were at Yankee and Shea stadiums, it was all just preliminary to the World Series.

Joe Torre, who grew up in Brooklyn and attended the last Subway Series in 1956 as a teenager, had managed both the Mets and Yankees. "Now it's more than just a baseball game," he said. "I hope the people behave themselves because this could break up some families."

A Mets-friendly priest told *The New York Times* that he never prayed for his club to win because "there could be a bishop praying on the other side." Politicians, looking to this World Series for every possible vote, had a slippery slope as well. Rick Lazio, a longtime Mets fan and New York's Republican candidate for the Senate, picked the Mets in seven. Opponent Hillary Clinton, favored over Lazio, was still lambasted in some corners for donning a Yankees cap when the world champs visited the White House a year earlier.

While New Yorkers went gaga over the intra-city classic, the rest of the country apparently yawned. The 12.4 television rating for the matchup was, at the time, the lowest in the history of televised World Series.

A Series Full of Comebacks

2001: Arizona 4, New York 3

The September 11 terrorist attacks on the United States prompted many to rethink the place of sports in our lives. Sports were a needed "escape," some claimed. Silly games, others contended, not as meaningful as they once seemed. Come World Series time, barely more than a month removed from the unthinkable tragedies, fans in the former camp had something on which to hang their rally caps: one of the most enthralling World Series of all time.

The mighty Yankees, cheered by "America's Mayor" Rudy Giuliani, were seeking their fourth consecutive championship and fifth in six years. They were opposed by an Arizona franchise that was in its fourth year of existence.

The Diamondbacks, however, had something none of the Yankees' recent World Series foes had possessed—two power-pitching aces in the rotation, Curt Schilling and Randy Johnson. The Yankees managed just three hits in

each of the first two games in Phoenix, falling 9-1 and 4-0. The series then moved to New York, where there would be an emotional tribute to those who had lost their lives in the World Trade Center attacks.

After President George W. Bush threw out the first pitch in Game 3, the Yankees inspired the city—indeed, the nation—with three unforgettable one-run wins in their home park. Roger Clemens and Mariano Rivera got things started with a 2-1, three-hit victory in Game 3. On Halloween night, New York was trailing 3-1 with two outs in the ninth inning of Game 4 when Tino Martinez blasted a game-tying, two-run homer off reliever Byung-Hyun Kim. Derek Jeter won it after midnight on a solo shot in the 10th inning, earning him the nickname "Mr. November."

Unbelievably, New York's Scott Brosius knotted Game 5 with a two-run, two-out homer in the ninth inning, also off the shell-shocked Kim. When Alfonso Soriano won the contest on a single in the 12th, the Diamondbacks had to

Scott Brosius's dramatic two-out, two-run homer tied Game 5 in the ninth inning and led to a Yankees win, but it only delayed Arizona's first championship celebration.

Above: The 2001 World Series was a battle between the 38-time pennant-winning Yankees and the first-time flag-winning Diamondbacks.

Left: One out from a Game 4 loss, Tino Martinez rescued the Yankees with a two-run, game-tying blast. Derek Jeter then won it for New York with a 10th-inning home run. Since the blast occurred after midnight on Halloween night, Jeter earned the nickname "Mr. November."

be thinking that the gods of baseball were wearing pinstripes.

"If you had told me, I wouldn't have believed it," Arizona's Reggie Sanders said after the game. "I wouldn't have believed it would happen the first time, let alone the second time. But they pulled it out. . . . They had that magic working for them again."

After Arizona returned to the desert and delivered a resounding 15-2 counterpunch in Game 6, the Diamondbacks had outscored the Yankees 34-12 to that point, yet they stood even with the three-time defending champs at three wins apiece. Given New York's championship experience, it seemed a winner-take-all final game might be the perfect setting for the Yankees to break through with the first road victory of the set.

Clemens, the AL Cy Young Award winner, opposed Schilling and yielded just one run. Schilling allowed two,

2001 World Series

Game 1						
NYY	100	000	000	1	3	2
ARZ	104	400	00x	9	10	0

Game 2						
NYY	000	000	000	0	3	0
ARZ	010	000	30x	4	5	0

Game 3						
ARZ	000	100	000	1	3	3
NYY	010	001	00x	2	7	1

Game 4						
ARZ	000	100	020 0	3	6	0
NYY	001	000	002 1	4	7	0

Game 5						
ARZ	000	020	000 000	2	8	0
NYY	000	000	002 001	3	9	1

Game 6						
NYY	000	002	000	2	7	1
ARZ	138	300	00x	15	22	0

Game 7						
NYY	000	000	110	2	6	3
ARZ	000	001	002	3	11	0

including Soriano's eighth-inning home run that put New York ahead 2-1. The Yankees then turned the game over to baseball's most dominant closer. Rivera had converted 23 consecutive postseason save opportunities. It was time for the champagne bottles to be readied in the visiting clubhouse.

Except, on this night, World Series magic belonged to Arizona.

Mark Grace led off with a single. Damian Miller put down a sacrifice bunt but reached base when Rivera overthrew second trying to get the lead runner. It was the third Yankees error of the game.

Jay Bell's bunt was not as successful, forcing an out at third, but Tony Womack doubled home the tying run. After Rivera hit Craig Counsell to load the bases, Luis Gonzalez delivered one of the most memorable hits in World Series history, blooping a single over Jeter's head to drive in Bell with the

Above: Derek Jeter lifts Chuck Knoblauch off his feet after Knoblauch scored the winning run in the 12th inning of Game 5 at Yankee Stadium. Rookie second baseman Alfonso Soriano had knocked home Knoblauch with a single.

"I think the people of New York got what they wanted.... They saw a baseball team that struggled at times yet found a way to get through tough situations. I think that pretty much epitomizes what they've been doing the last couple of months. I think we picked up the personality and inspiration of New York."

—Yankees manager Joe Torre

winning run and put the exclamation point on a dramatic duel.

"I'm just proud to be part of one of the greatest World Series in the history of the game," Grace said after a series that featured an amazing three ninth-inning comebacks. "And I don't think anybody would argue with me on that."

Schilling and Johnson were named co-MVPs. Johnson earned three of Arizona's victories and Schilling the other, and each posted an ERA well below 2.00.

Giuliani made the trip to Phoenix for Game 7 along with a group of Yankees fans who had lost relatives in the 9/11 attacks. After Arizona secured the win, Giuliani, the lifelong Yankees fan, stood and applauded. It was that kind of World Series.

Above: Mariano Rivera entered the ninth inning of Game 7 with a 2-1 lead. But after a single, error, double, hit-by-pitch, and bloop single by Luis Gonzalez, Arizona won the series.

THE EMOTIONS OF 9/11

The grim and bloody terrorist attacks against the United States on September 11, 2001, sent the entire nation into a tailspin of shock, grief, and anger such had never been seen or felt before. Nowhere was that emotional brickbat felt more keenly than in the proud heart of urban America, New York City, the site of the two deadliest attacks.

Major League Baseball shut down for a week after the terrible day and pushed its schedule back. When the games resumed, New Yorkers seemed to reach out and find some solace in a beloved pastime. Twelve days after the attacks, Yankee Stadium was the site of a special program, "A Prayer for America," which featured James Earl Jones and Oprah Winfrey as emcees along with dozens of religious and political figures, singers and instrumentalists, and New York City firefighters and policemen. When Bette Midler sang "Wind Beneath My Wings" ("Did I ever tell you you're my hero?"), many people who had lost loved ones in the attacks cried heavy tears.

A different kind of powerful moment occurred before Game 3 of that year's World Series, when President George W. Bush strode out to the pitcher's mound in Yankee Stadium to throw out the game's ceremonial first pitch. Bush himself said, "I have never felt anything like that in my life." Commentators, historians, and everyday people were deeply moved by the incredible energy. One of the many homemade signs that hung from Yankee Stadium's railings summed up the overriding sentiment: "USA fears nobody. Play ball." Bush gave a thumbs-up, wound up, and fired a strike.

Yankees fans in the aftermath of 9/11

MARLINS SWIM OFF WITH THE TITLE

2003: Florida 4, New York 2

The 2003 World Series pitted the New York Yankees, a championship-tested team of veterans, against a Florida Marlins club that began the season at 19-29, pulled a 72-year-old manager out of retirement to right the ship, and struggled to draw fans to attend its own games. Yet this series was no mismatch. The 11-year-old Marlins, just as they had in 1997 (the only other year they finished with a winning record), celebrated a World Series championship come October.

"When you're that young, you don't know what fear is," Yankees manager Joe Torre said, referring to World Series MVP Josh Beckett. He could have been talking about any number of the Marlins, who continually came through in the clutch while the Yankees struggled to do the same.

After getting to the World Series with a Game 7 victory over the rival Red Sox in the American League Championship Series, the Bronx Bombers had the bats taken out of their hands by a young Marlins staff that rose to the grand occasion. Hard-throwing 25-year-old Brad Penny won Games 1 and 5 by scores of 3-2 and 6-4. In between, the Yankees got back-to-back 6-1 wins from Andy Pettitte and Mike Mussina, but Game 4 was the pivotal game.

The Marlins led the fourth contest 3-1 entering the ninth inning at Pro Player Stadium, but Yankees pinch hitter Ruben Sierra smacked a two-run triple off closer Ugueth Urbina to tie the score. Florida, though, was no stranger to such games. The Marlins had made a habit of pulling out victory in their final at-bat. In fact, they had come from behind in both Games 6 and 7 of the NLCS to defeat the Cubs. So it came as little surprise when Alex Gonzalez, 26, ripped the winning home run down the left-field line off Jeff Weaver in the 12th inning to even the series.

After Penny's Game 5 pitching put Florida on the brink of its second championship, Beckett strode into the

Josh Beckett helps his own cause by chasing down Jorge Posada for the final out of Game 6 of the 2003 World Series. Beckett was voted series MVP after firing a shutout in this clinching game.

2003 World Series

Game 1

FLA	100 020 000	3 7 1
NYY	001 001 000	2 9 0

Game 2

FLA	000 000 001	1 6 0
NYY	310 200 00x	6 10 2

Game 3

NYY	000 100 014	6 6 1
FLA	100 000 000	1 8 0

Game 4

NYY	010 000 002 000	3 12 0
FLA	300 000 000 001	4 10 0

Game 5

NYY	100 000 102	4 12 1
FLA	030 120 00x	6 9 1

Game 6

FLA	000 011 000	2 7 0
NYY	000 000 000	0 5 1

spotlight. The 23-year-old took the Yankee Stadium mound for Game 6 and pitched the 19th deciding-game shutout in World Series history, 2-0. In two series starts, Beckett allowed just two earned runs over 16 ⅓ innings, striking out 19 against five walks.

"This guy is special," said Jack McKeon, the veteran manager who came out of the shadows to guide the Marlins to the top. "This guy has the guts of a burglar. He's mentally tough. I knew he had the confidence to go out there and do the job."

The Yankees outscored the Marlins 21-17 in the six games. They outhit Florida by nearly 30 points, and they smashed six homers to the Marlins' two, with Bernie Williams clubbing a pair himself. Williams collected 10 hits in the series and Jeter nine, more than any player on the Marlins. It didn't matter, because Florida was better when it counted.

"They have got 26 championships, and we wanted to play them," Beckett said. "Because if you are going to beat somebody, why not beat the best?"

Above: Bernie Williams homers in the first game of the 2003 World Series, in which batted he .400. When he left the Yankees in 2006, Williams held major league postseason records for games (121), doubles (29), RBI (80), and extra-base hits (51).

Opposite page, below: Marlins players wait at home plate for Alex Gonzalez, whose 12th-inning homer off a dejected Jeff Weaver decided Game 4 in Miami. The Yankees had scored two runs in the ninth inning to tie it.

Right: Two years after losing to the Diamondbacks in the World Series, the Yankees fell to yet another upstart expansion team in the Florida Marlins.

Dubbed "Mr. November" for his heroics in the first-ever November World Series game in 2001, Derek Jeter has shined in November *and* October throughout his long career. Jeter arrived in 1996, just as the Yankees were beginning a postseason roll that turned the shortstop into an October fixture. As the longest-tenured everyday Yankee during an era with a three-tiered playoff format, he has amassed numbers that no one else has approached.

Entering 2010, Jeter held MLB postseason records for games (138), at-bats (559), hits (175), and total bases (268). In those 138 games—against quality pitching, in hand-numbing weather, and under intense pressure—he hit .313 with 20 home runs and 99 runs scored, which is also a post-season record.

Derek Jeter

YANKS, "CORE FOUR" BACK ON TOP

2009: New York 4, Philadelphia 2

Four. It's the number of games required to win a World Series. And it's the number of Yankees who, in 2009, did precisely that for the fifth time in pinstripes.

Some players revel in reaching the top once in a career, and well they should. When you're a Yankee, expectations run higher. And no one enjoyed the satisfaction of putting baseball back on its axis with the Yankees' first title since 2000 like the "Core Four" of Derek Jeter, Jorge Posada, Andy Pettitte, and Mariano Rivera.

"It's back where it belongs," Jeter said, pointing to the club's 27th World Series trophy after knocking off the defending champion Phillies in six games.

"To be able to play with those bunch of guys," Rivera said, "it's like working for a company with four people for your whole career. God bless those guys. Wonderful."

The Core Four began their run in 1996, when the Yankees won their first of four crowns in five years. From 2001 to 2008, they won two more American League pennants, but the Diamondbacks and Marlins denied them the grand prize.

After dropping Game 1 of the 2009 World Series 6-1 to Philadelphia, in New York, the Yankees turned to the stellar pitching and clutch hitting that had carried them to 103 wins during the regular season. A. J. Burnett and Pettitte made consecutive solid starts, and Hideki Matsui homered in each contest as the Yankees won 3-1 and 8-5 in Games 2 and 3. Three runs in the ninth inning of Game 4 broke a 4-4 tie and produced a 7-4 win in Philadelphia. Alex Rodriguez drove in the winning run with a final-inning double before Posada added a two-run, insurance single in the dramatic finish.

Now, just one win stood between the Core Four and a fifth ring. It did not come in Game 5, when the Phillies sprinted to a 6-1 lead and held on for an 8-6 triumph. But Yankee Stadium—the *new* Yankee Stadium—awaited a fate

Yankees first baseman Mark Teixeira records the last out of the 2009 World Series. It was Teixeira's first world title in pinstripes and the fifth for the "Core Four."

the old Yankee Stadium had become accustomed to since its opening in 1923.

Fittingly, the Yankees veterans played key roles in the clinching 7-3 win. Pettitte started and earned the victory, his fourth triumph of the postseason without a loss. Rivera recorded the final five outs. And Jeter went 3-for-5, capping another brilliant World Series performance with a .407 batting average.

Jeter would have been a terrific choice as World Series MVP were it not for Matsui, who drove in six runs in Game 6 and belted three home runs in the series. He finished with a showy .615 average, a 1.385 slugging percentage, and eight RBI to claim the award.

"It's an honor for me to win a championship with those guys," New York first baseman Mark Teixeira said of his veteran teammates. "They are Yankee legends."

"It feels better than I remember it, man," Jeter said. "It's been a long time."

Above: Hideki Matsui delivers two of his six Game 6 RBI on a second-inning home run. Matsui earned series MVP honors thanks to three homers and a gaudy .615 batting average.

"They're partying in Tokyo tonight!"

—Nick Swisher, after fellow Yankees outfielder Hideki Matsui drove in six runs in the World Series finale

Right: Some two million New Yorkers honored the Yankees during a 2009 victory parade. "Having been nine years," said Yankees managing partner Hal Steinbrenner, "you forget how magical this is."

Below: Alex Rodriguez awaits a replay review of his Game 3 home run in Philadelphia—a call that went his way. A-Rod amassed six home runs and 18 RBI in 15 postseason games in 2009.

When the Yankees acquired Alex Rodriguez on February 16, 2004, they anticipated more 40-homer seasons (he was coming off six in a row with Seattle and Texas) and at least one world championship. Voluntarily moving to third base, A-Rod continued to put up massive regular-season numbers (including a .314-54-156 MVP season in 2007), but his alleged rift with teammates was all over the media.

More troubles followed. The Yankees were ousted from three straight AL Division Series (2005-07), as Rodriguez totaled just one RBI in the 13 games. He re-upped with the Yankees for 10 years at $275 million, then New York didn't even make the playoffs in 2008. Early the next year, he was forced to address accusations of steroid use. A-Rod admitted to taking performance-enhancing drugs earlier in his career, although he said he had stopped using steroids before becoming a Yankee. "All my years in New York have been clean," he said.

The slugger's performance on the last day of the 2009 regular season (two homers and seven RBI in one inning) presaged a charmed October. Rodriguez batted .455 in the ALDS, hit .425 in the ALCS, and doubled in the ninth inning to help beat the Phillies in Game 4 of the World Series. Finally, A-Rod had given the Yankees what they had paid him for: a world title.

YANKEES IN THE WORLD SERIES

Yankees World Series Batting Leaders

Games

Yogi Berra	75
Mickey Mantle	65
Hank Bauer	53
Gil McDougald	53
Phil Rizzuto	52
Joe DiMaggio	51
Elston Howard	47
Bill Dickey	38
Derek Jeter	38
Tony Kubek	37

Batting Average
(50 at-bats minimum)

Reggie Jackson	.400
Thurman Munson	.373
Lou Gehrig	.361
Earle Combs	.350
Babe Ruth	.347
Billy Martin	.333
Derek Jeter	.321
Lou Piniella	.319
Gene Woodling	.318
Scott Brosius	.314

Runs

Mickey Mantle	42
Yogi Berra	41
Babe Ruth	37
Derek Jeter	32
Lou Gehrig	30
Joe DiMaggio	27
Elston Howard	25
Gil McDougald	23
Hank Bauer	21
Phil Rizzuto	21
Gene Woodling	21

Hits

Yogi Berra	71
Mickey Mantle	59
Joe DiMaggio	54
Derek Jeter	50
Hank Bauer	46
Gil McDougald	45
Phil Rizzuto	45
Lou Gehrig	43
Babe Ruth	41
Elston Howard	40
Bobby Richardson	40

Doubles

Yogi Berra	10
Derek Jeter	9
Lou Gehrig	8
Elston Howard	7
Clete Boyer	6
Jerry Coleman	6
Joe DiMaggio	6
Mickey Mantle	6
Bob Meusel	6
Paul O'Neill	6
Bobby Richardson	6

Triples

Billy Johnson	4
Hank Bauer	3
Bobby Brown	3
Lou Gehrig	3
Billy Martin	3
Bob Meusel	3

Home Runs

Mickey Mantle	18
Babe Ruth	15
Yogi Berra	12
Lou Gehrig	10
Joe DiMaggio	8
Reggie Jackson	8
Hank Bauer	7
Gil McDougald	7
Bill Skowron	7
Bill Dickey	5
Elston Howard	5
Charlie Keller	5
Roger Maris	5
Billy Martin	5
Bernie Williams	5

RBI

Mickey Mantle	40
Yogi Berra	39
Lou Gehrig	35
Joe DiMaggio	30
Babe Ruth	30
Bill Skowron	26
Hank Bauer	24
Bill Dickey	24
Gil McDougald	24
Tony Lazzeri	19
Billy Martin	19

Stolen Bases

Phil Rizzuto	10
Bob Meusel	5
Derek Jeter	4
Babe Ruth	4
Mickey Mantle	3
Mickey Rivers	3

Yankees World Series Pitching Leaders

Wins

Whitey Ford	10
Allie Reynolds	7
Red Ruffing	7
Lefty Gomez	6
Waite Hoyt	6
Andy Pettitte	5
Herb Pennock	5
Vic Raschi	5
Eddie Lopat	4
Monte Pearson	4
Bob Turley	4

Innings

Whitey Ford	146.0
Red Ruffing	85.2
Waite Hoyt	77.2
Andy Pettitte	71.2
Allie Reynolds	77.1
Vic Raschi	60.1

Right: Yogi Berra (*top left*) with (*clockwise*) Mickey Mantle, Vic Raschi, and Allie Reynolds

Bob Turley	53.2
Herb Pennock	52.1
Eddie Lopat	52.0
Lefty Gomez	50.1

Strikeouts

Whitey Ford	94
Allie Reynolds	62
Red Ruffing	61
Andy Pettitte	56
Waite Hoyt	48
Bob Turley	46
Vic Raschi	43
Roger Clemens	37

ERA

(30 innings minimum)

Mariano Rivera	0.99
Monte Pearson	1.01
Roger Clemens	1.50
Spud Chandler	1.62
Waite Hoyt	1.62
Ron Guidry	1.69
Herb Pennock	2.06
Vic Raschi	2.24
Carl Mays	2.38

Saves

Mariano Rivera	11
Johnny Murphy	4
Allie Reynolds	4
John Wetteland	4
Herb Pennock	3
Rich Gossage	2
Bob Kuzava	2
Joe Page	2

Yankees World Series MVPs

(since 1955, first year of the award)

Don Larsen, 1956
Bob Turley, 1958
Bobby Richardson, 1960
Whitey Ford, 1961
Ralph Terry, 1962
Reggie Jackson, 1977
Bucky Dent, 1978
John Wetteland, 1996
Scott Brosius, 1998
Mariano Rivera, 1999
Derek Jeter, 2000
Hideki Matsui, 2009

Yankees World Series "Dream Team"

1B Lou Gehrig (.361/.477/.731, 10 HRs, 35 RBI, 21 XBH, 30 runs in 34 games)

2B Gil McDougald (7 HRs, 24 RBI in 53 games)

SS Derek Jeter (.321/.384/.449, 32 runs, 50 hits in 38 games)

3B Red Rolfe (.284, 17 runs, 33 hits in 28 games)

OF Babe Ruth (.347/.493/.788, 15 HRs, 30 RBI, 37 runs in 36 games)

OF Mickey Mantle (18 HRs, 40 RBI, 42 runs, 43 BBs, 123 TBs in 65 games)

OF Reggie Jackson (.400/.500/.891, 8 HRs in 15 games)

C Yogi Berra (all-time MLB WS leader: 75 games, 71 hits, 49 singles, 10 doubles)

RHP Red Ruffing (7-2, 2.63 ERA, 85.2 IP, 61 Ks, 8 CGs)

LHP Whitey Ford (10-8, 2.71 ERA, 146 IP, 7 CGs, 3 SHOs)

CL Mariano Rivera (0.99 ERA, 24 games, 36.1 IP, 8 BBs, 32 Ks, 11 saves)

INDEX

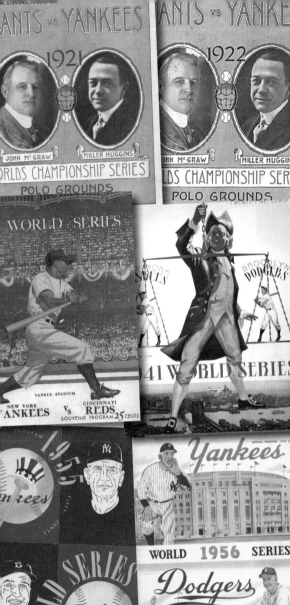

ANTS vs YANKEES
1921
JOHN McGRAW · MILLER HUGGINS
WORLDS CHAMPIONSHIP SERIES
POLO GROUNDS

ANTS vs YANKEES
1922
JOHN McGRAW · MILLER HUGGINS
WORLDS CHAMPIONSHIP SERIES
POLO GROUNDS

ANKEES vs GIANTS
1923
MILLER HUGGINS · JOHN McGRAW
WORLDS CHAMPIONSHIP SERIES
NEW YORK CITY

Cardinals vs. Yankees
for the Championship of the World
1926
Official Score Card
Price 25¢

YANKEES vs PIRA
1927
MILLER HUGGINS
WORLDS CHAMPIONS

WORLD SERIES
YANKEE STADIUM
NEW YORK ANKEES vs CINCINNATI REDS
SOUVENIR PROGRAM 25 CENTS

YORK NTS · BROOKLYN DODGERS
'41 WORLD SERIES

1942 WORLD SERIES
Buy WAR BONDS AND STAMPS
NEW YORK YANKEES · ST. LOUIS CARDINALS

1943 WORLD SERIES
NEW YORK YANKEES / ST. LOUIS CARDINALS

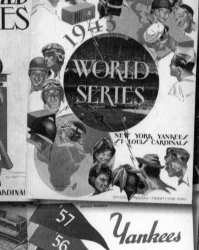
1921 · 1922
1923 · 1926
1928 · 1932
1937 · 1938
1941 · 1942
19 Yankees
WORLD SER
BROOKLYN DO

1955
Yankees
WORLD SERIES
Dodgers

Yankees
YANKEE STADIUM
WORLD 1956 SERIES
Dodgers

Yankees
1942-1923
1942-1943 1941
1926-1927 1947-1949
1931-1932 1950-1951
1936-1937 1952-1953
1938-1939 1955-1956
"Home of Champions"
1957
NEW YORK   MILWAUKEE
Yankees Braves
WORLD 1957 SERIES

'57 '56 '55 '53 '52 '51 '50 '49 '47 '43 '42
Yankees vs. MILWAUKEE Braves
1958 WORLD SERIES

WORLD SERIES
NEW YORK YAN
PITTSBURGH PIRA

World Series 1977

1978 WORLD SERIES
CHAMPIONS

WORLD SERIES 1981
NATIONAL LEAGUE AMERICAN LEAGUE

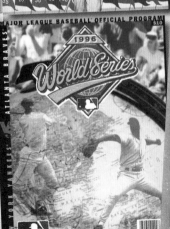
1996 World Series
ATLANTA BRAVES
MAJOR LEAGUE BASEBALL OFFICIAL PROGRAM

World Series
THE FALL